MW00977128

THE
POWER of
Passion, Courage, & Faith

Your Life, Your Joy, Your Way

ROSALYN TAYLOR O'NEALE

Llumina
PRESS

Editor's note:

The names, details, and circumstances may have been changed to protect the privacy of those mentioned in this publication.

ISBN: 978-1-62550-215-5

Printed in the United States of America by Llumina Press

TABLE OF CONTENTS

DEDICATION

To know anything about me is to know my mother, Katherine Estelle Taylor Smith. Everything that I am and all that I know are the results of her love, laughter, and insanity. She taught me to live a passionate life, to act with courage, and to believe in God, friends and strangers, and myself.

Helping others was her gift, her passion, and it showed in everyday random acts of kindness. She was a social worker who brought children to our house for the weekend so their mothers, who were welfare recipients, could, as she said, "Find a way to get food in the house and make sure the kids have clean clothes by Sunday night." The children came to know her as Aunt Katherine, and throughout her life, they would return to our home to share pictures of their graduations, weddings, and children. She taught special education, and was often one of the first people for many of her students to hug them and tell them she loved them —and mean it.

I remember a twelve-year-old (we were the same age) who at age three was severely burned when her mother intentionally put her head in a hot oven and held the door closed. People often looked away when they saw Jena, but my mother gently touched her face and told her how lovely she looked. I will never forget the last hour of Jena's life. While we were on a school outing with mom's students, Jena committed suicide. She scaled a fence, climbed the diving board, and jumped into deep water, knowing she could not swim. After they pulled Jena's body from the water, I saw my mother, tears running down her face, holding Jena's head in her lap, gently stroking her face and telling her how beautiful she was.

Mom taught me that service to others often required courage. She fought the welfare system. She believed that given a chance, resources, and support, women who lived through the abuse and the dysfunction of generational welfare could become college graduates and productive and contributing citizens. When colleagues gave up on people, Katherine believed in them and fought for their right to be treated with dignity and respect.

My mom was as faithful as she was fearless. She taught me to have faith in myself. She showed me what belief looked like and how it felt. She was living proof that cancer, meningitis, a quadruple bypass, gallstones, a car fire, welfare systems, and impersonal educational systems could not defeat her. She made me believe that nothing could get the better of me unless I let it.

She had faith in the goodness of others. She said that given the chance, people would help each other. It might be changing a flat tire, helping to feed a family whose home was destroyed by fire, or giving someone a second chance and a job. It could be as easy as providing lunch money for a first-grader or as challenging as getting a young woman into college.

She had a deep and unshakable belief in God, more than the Sundays we spent in the fourth-row pew at Church of Our Merciful Savior (the same one her father and my grandfather Francis Taylor sat on). It was more than the blessing of the food. She knew that God could and did do miracles. She believed that God was always with her and that, with Him on her side, she could do anything. She taught me the living, breathing meaning of unconditional Divine love.

Anyone who met her can remember a funny story or memory that made him or her laugh aloud and filled their eyes with tears. She gave me the gift of her laughter and taught me to pass it on. The hole her death left in the hearts of those who knew her is large, but it is minuscule compared to the love and the joy she brought to our lives. She was and is for me the living, breathing example of the power of passion, courage, and faith.

PREFACE

I was standing on the side of the stage, preparing to "ask" an audience of one thousand well-dressed, well-to-do women and men to open their purses and wallets and donate money. My "ask" always followed a client story, the segment in the evening when a woman shared the personal journey that brought her to the stage of the Grand Hyatt Hotel in New York City.

Year after year, these brave women (most of whom were not public speakers) shared a journey that frequently began in desperate situations, fueled by poverty and abuse, and often led to unimaginable violence and indescribable loss. In the end, these warrior women found their way to Dress for Success[1], and with determined spirits and lots of helping hands, they triumphed over tragedies and obstacles many of us cannot imagine. They walked victoriously to the podium and shared their stories of pain and success.

Although I knew the stories ended well (that's why they were on the stage), they were extremely painful to hear. There was the story about the seventeen-year-old woman-child who ran away from an abusive home in Colorado seeking a new life of unlimited possibilities. She got off the bus in New York City, and three days later began a decades-long journey into hell after being kidnapped, raped, beaten, imprisoned, and forced into prostitution.

Or the story shared by a woman with a master's degree in social work (like me) from Louisville, Kentucky (like me), who drove while under the influence of alcohol (like me), and in a freak car accident killed her best friend. She spent the next seven years in prison for vehicular homicide. When she left prison, she had lost her home, marriage, children, job, and her best friend.

What all the women who stood on the stages had in common was that they once dreamed of being someone other than who they were when they were walking the streets or sitting in their prison cell. As I listened to their stories, I felt a deep need to say something to the millions of women with similarly damaged beginnings and middles, who had *not* made it out. I began to write *Passion, Courage, and Faith* for all those who felt that the window of possibility for happiness, joy, and peace was permanently nailed shut. I wanted to give them an opening through which they could run, walk, or crawl.

I started by asking questions. I spoke with women at conferences, in hotel lobbies, on planes, and at bus stops. I challenged anyone who would listen to think about what they loved doing and to ask themselves what it would take to pursue it. I needed to understand how and why some women ended up on the stage sharing their stories and others on the streets asking for spare change. As I talked and listened, I was struck by two themes: women who found their passion seemed happier than those who did not, and it took courage to move from prison to the podium.

I shared what I was thinking and learning and two things happened. Women grabbed me in the hotel years after we first met to tell me how our conversation led them to start a business or pursue their education. They called or sent emails about how something they heard me say caused them to pause, and many said it led them to see new possibilities.

Second, I realized I wanted and needed to share what I discovered about the power of finding one's voice, one's passion, and having the courage to go from being afraid to being willing to try. I silenced the voices that told me I wasn't good enough or didn't have enough research and began to write *Passion, Courage, and Faith*. It has taken ten years to bring this from a question to a few answers.

I know there are men traveling similar paths, but I have spent most of my life talking with and listening to women: my mother, my daughters, lovers, friends, women on welfare, and women on corporate boards. This makes it easier for me to relate to the issues women face and offer things that have worked for me and other women I know.

This story is not based on years of groundbreaking scientific research. There are plenty of those on the shelves at your local bookstore. *Passion, Courage, and Faith* is the result of conversations with hundreds of women I met while traveling across six continents. Sometimes it was a group of women sitting around the dining room table, sharing the stories of their struggles with addiction, body image, and hot flashes. Sometimes we laughed; often we cried, reached across the table to pat a woman's hand, or searched our purse for a tissue to give to a sister-friend whose tears of pain or joy rolled down her face.

Many times, the conversations were one-on-one, with women I had known for years and others I just met. We talked about how sometimes life brought us to a place of peace—more often to a place we did not recognize and could not have imagined—sometimes magical, often horrific.

It is important to note that I spoke with women who *did* spend almost every day doing work (and play) they love. Their stories gave me and those I shared them with a renewed hope. They proved that living a joy-filled life doing what we love was possible. However, the vast majority of women I met described a life of doing what they had to do to survive and not what they loved. They worked (if they were lucky) at jobs that dulled their souls and broke their spirits.

I wrote *Passion, Courage, and Faith* for my daughters, Denita and Danielle, my granddaughter Denisha, and for all the women and girls who don't believe they can live their dreams. This book is an exploration of how I aligned my heart and work with divine purpose. It is a road map for dreaming with a plan to get to your destination. I talk about the good days and the bad ones, the valleys of depression, and life on the top of the mountain.

We can always write the book that details life's failures and disappointments. Maybe the goal should be to explore how we can have and live a blessed life filled with good times, deep and lasting friendships, and an abundance of love. If this is one of your goals, the words on these pages can help.

Passion, Courage, and Faith is for all women—those who have discovered the rainbow and those who live under the clouds, worried about rain and bad hair days. I hope women share these strategies with the men they love, but I'm writing it for you, the housewife who once dreamed of being a painter and struggles every day with issues of weight and worth. It is for the incarcerated woman, whose picture of her six-year-old self, dancing around her bedroom, is now taped to her prison wall.

I don't think I have the answers and will now "impart them to you." Not even close. When I live in alignment with my God, I begin and end most days feeling joyful. Spiritual leader Wayne Dyer said, "If you're uncomfortable with the term God, just add an 'o' and make it Good. It's the same thing."

Many women I've met see their daily struggle as the road map of their life and not a momentary detour. If you are one of these women, *Passion, Courage, and Faith* is for you. It is a practical, empowering, and easy-to-follow workbook, incorporating stories, strategies, and exercises to help you, the reader, find a way to *your* destination, *your* life, *your* joy, *your* way.

Here are my stories and those of the many women and men I've met along my journey. I hope that something on these pages will make you smile or laugh and compel you to pick up the paintbrush, put down the donut, or write the proposal.

INTRODUCTION

Have you ever wished you could live the life that Oprah[2] lives? You know, the life where someone takes care of all the crappy things like hair and makeup, every day you do what you love for throngs of adoring fans, and people pay you huge amounts of money? That's probably not going to happen, but *Passion, Courage, and Faith* can make it easier to have a rich, full, and enjoyable life doing what brings you joy and happiness.

It is written for the woman who wants more (or less) in her life and feels like an Israelite wandering around Mount Sinai for forty years, even if it's only been six months. It is for the thirty-four-year-old accounting supervisor who once dreamed of performing on the Broadway stage or singing at the Apollo. On good days, she serenades her cats while cleaning the hair from the bathroom sink. It's for the woman who spent her first twenty years abusing substances and her soul and who is ready for a very different next twenty-year journey.

Throughout the book, I will introduce you to women I met before and during its writing. Unless I specify, the women named here are a collection of women I met and any resemblance to actual people is coincidental. At the end of each chapter, there are questions that will help you listen to and honor your voice.

I know this book is long. You don't have to read it from beginning to end; you can search for pages that resonate with you where you are today. This is a journey. Read as many pages as you feel like today and come back to it when you're ready. Don't read this the way you think you "should." Let the Universe lead you.

Chapter 1 focuses on your gift and passion – finding your gift and nourishing it.

Chapter 2 will help you find the courage to pursue your passion.

Passion and courage can only get you so far. You need a plan.

Chapter 3 – "The First Key: The Worthy Goal" sets the stage.

Chapter 4 – "The Second Key: Behave like You Mean It" focuses on aligning your words and your walk.

Chapter 5 – "The Third Key: Gather Guides and Supporters" directs you to find people who will shine a light on the path and lift you up when you stumble

Chapter 6 – "The Fourth Key: Learn Everything" looks at the importance of expanding your knowledge.

Chapter 7 – "The Fifth Key: Are We There Yet?" looks at goals, measurements, and metrics.

Chapter 8 – "The Sixth Key: Involve Everyone" helps you identify ways to engage friends, family, strangers, and the people they know.

In Chapters 9-11, I share how faith in oneself, in others, and in a higher power (God, Allah, Buddha, the Universe) can provide the light that follows the darkness.

Chapter 12 – "From Seed to Blossoms" contains my final thoughts and advice.

This book is not for everyone. If you're confident that you are living your most passionate and courageous life, put this book down. If you get up every day knowing that you and your calling are in sync and you continue to move forward even when you're unsure and afraid, you don't need help.

People often ask for proof that if they follow the path I describe in this book they will be successful. Before investing so much time and energy, they want to see evidence that their efforts will result in extraordinary achievements, but no matter how much proof I offer, at some point you have to take a leap and believe that following this path will get you closer to your destination than wandering alone.

For those still reading, I wish I could say that I've applied every principle on these pages and achieved all of my goals, but that would be a lie. Nevertheless, friends, family, and colleagues reported that when they had something they wanted to achieve, *Passion, Courage, and Faith* was an invaluable resource.

"No, this is not the beginning of a new chapter in my life; this is the beginning of a new book! That first book is already closed, ended, and tossed into the seas; this new book is newly opened, has just begun! Look, it is the first page! And it is a beautiful one!"

– C. Joy Bell C

PART I:

The Power in You

THE BEGINNING EXERCISE

Take ten to twenty minutes without distraction. (do this instead of watching the woman on The Maury Show™ fall on the floor after she can't identify her baby-daddy for the 11th time). Write whatever comes to mind in the boxes below. Don't worry if it seems impossible or "'stupid'." Calm the demons and listen to that small quiet voice that knows your heart.

What do I want to change (e.g., marital status, health profile, financial picture)?

What do I wish I had (e.g., a job I enjoy, patience, health, children)? Or wish I didn't have (e.g., a bad temper, cellulite, stress)?

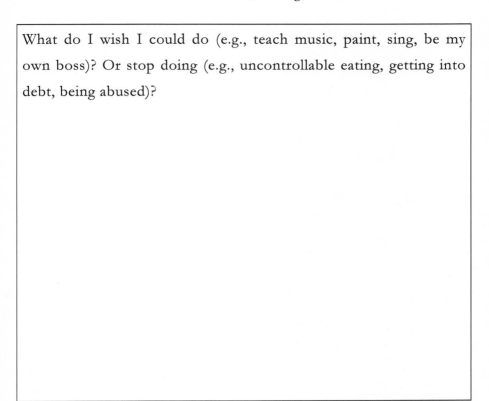

What do I wish I could do (e.g., teach music, paint, sing, be my own boss)? Or stop doing (e.g., uncontrollable eating, getting into debt, being abused)?

Having trouble? Ask yourself, "If I was free from fear, worry, and self-doubt, what would I write in the boxes above?" Now go back and answer the questions as if you were a free woman, because you are.

CHAPTER 1

LIVE PASSIONATELY

"And the day came when the risk it took to remain tight in the bud was greater than the risk it took to blossom."[4]

—Anais Nin

DISCOVERING THE GIFT

"I do not at all understand the mystery of grace - only that it meets us where we are but does not leave us where it found us."

Everyone has a gift given by the Divinity. This is the major premise of *Passion, Courage, and Faith.* I love what the author of FindYourDivineGift.com says: "It seems like just before we slip down the slide into this human life we are handed a note on which is written a unique gift for us to share with the world."[5] Today your note comes with the following instructions: Use, enjoy, cherish, and honor your gift.

Throughout this book, the seed symbolizes that gift. In nature, seeds contain the roots, the berries, flowers, and the trees. In *Passion, Courage, and Faith,* the seed contains the outward symbols—the paintings, songs, businesses, or lifestyle—the things that bring you joy and make you smile. Everything we want to be is contained in the divine seed, and therefore in us.

When we are young, the seed appears in our dreams of doing work that changes the world or our community, acquiring wealth or status, or creating beautiful things. For some, the seed is the hope of athletic prowess, saving lives, or inventing something great—the next "must have." For others, it may be leading or inspiring those who are lost, ashamed, or just beginning their journeys.

As Paulo Coelho says in *The Alchemist,* "Everyone, when they are young knows what their Personal Legend is. At that point in their lives, everything is clear and everything is possible. They are not afraid to dream, and to yearn for everything they would like to see happen to them in their lives."[6]

Years pass, and as we grow older, many of us lose the spiritual freedom to dream and see the possibilities. Being an adult is physically and mentally draining and often leaves little time to tend to the musings from our childhood. Decades later, finding that seed can be a difficult task—the garden where our dreams are planted receives less water and light and eventually goes dormant. When I started this journey, I was surprised at the response I got when I asked, "What is your gift?"

Many women replied, "I don't have one."

Because I didn't believe that, I asked another question. "If you had unlimited resources (time, money, freedom) and an unwavering belief that you have the right to be happy, what would you do?"

Without hesitation women responded. "I would paint, sing, dance, open a business, teach, learn, and travel to India and Africa." The list was amazing. The answers came easily and freely.

What, I wondered, makes claiming our gift so difficult?

It turns out that for many of us, guilt, shame, or a lack of worthiness causes us to deny that there is something we would love to do, be, have, give, or get. Many women do not believe they are worthy of their gifts, so they deny they have one. I was convinced that in each of us is something we are gifted to do, and I set out to prove it.

First, I had to define what it looked like, when it first appeared, how you could recognize it, if it grew or changed, and if, once it appeared, was ever lost. I discovered that the gift could take as many forms as there are people.

The seed may contain music, as it does in my grandson, Dylan. From the time he first picked up a guitar, it was clear that his gift, the divine seed in him, showed in the music that soothed and healed his wounds and brought joy to those of us blessed to hear him.

My gift is one of the greatest fears for most people—public speaking, telling stories to strangers and friends, groups of any size, persuasion, or demographic. I drove my mother to distraction with my constant chatter. My first- through sixth-grade report cards contained the same narrative: "Rosalyn is a good student, but she talks too much."

My favorite therapist said I could talk a dog off a meat truck, and it was true. I talked my way into and out of precarious situations. I talked people into doing things with me that their parents would never have allowed. I talked teachers into giving me more time to finish projects, principals out of suspending me for violations (except for one incident of drunkenness on school property), and neighbors into buying whatever I was selling.

At eighteen, I got my first master of ceremonies job at a citywide celebration. The challenge was to get strangers to stop eating meat on a stick and listen to the speakers. I was a moderately attractive, young Black woman with a loud and distinct voice. I was also fearless. I remember the thrill of watching people walk past, and then stop to listen to what I was saying.

I've heard people say, "At that moment, I knew..." and I, like many of you, have been skeptical. But the truth is that standing on that stage talking to strolling strangers felt as natural as drinking from a cup, and I knew my calling. I knew that I would talk for free, and for years, that's exactly what I did. The physical rewards were gold-plated clocks, etched glass book weights, and leather binders. In truth, the reward was the look on people's faces as I spoke or shared stories. It is magical.

This was my divine gift—the seed that held the roots, the leaves, and the flowers that would eventually grow into my vocation and avocation. I had unearthed my seed of greatness.

Have you? If not, read on.

A seed, in order to grow and bear fruit or flowers, requires three things—soil, water, and light, or in the language of this book, passion, courage, and faith. The first step is removing all the dead leaves covering your divine gift. This is not your mother's gift—it is your gift. The task is to find the soil that will allow it to grow from the tiniest seed to a towering willow.

BE YOU; YOU'RE GOOD AT IT

"Comparison is the thief of happiness."[7]

Over the years, there has always been someone I wanted to be. In high school, I wanted to be Michelle, the head cheerleader, dating the handsome and charming William. She filled a bra in ways that I still can't. I was smart, but she was smarter. I had friends; she had the school.

Fast-forward forty years. I'm watching the Hawaii Ironman Triathlon. It's a 2.4-mile swim, 112-mile bike ride, and a full 26.2-mile marathon. The TV network follows several "average" people from training to the victorious finish.

I always focus on one person. This year it is Joan, a woman my age competing in her first Ironman. They show her on her early morning swims, afternoon rides, and Sunday runs. I see her leave her home in Washington and arrive in Hawaii. I follow her journey to the starting line.

Cameras show her three sons and two grandchildren clapping excitedly as her number is written on her leg and arm. When I watch this ritual, I think, "That's how they would be able to identify my body when they pulled it from the water."

I cheer along with her friends and the strangers who line the roads. Throughout the day, I follow her progress and learn interesting tidbits about her life. She stares into the camera and tells the world that she always believed that someday she would do this, and although friends and family said it was impossible, it was as Paulo says in *The Alchemist*, her "legend."[8]

Somewhere around the third hour of the competition, I realize I want the crowds cheering for me. I want my grandchildren to hold up signs as I cross the finish line. I want my friends to surround me with hugs and tears. I want to be that woman, but—and this is important—I don't want to do what she had to do to get here.

The first leg of the triathlon is a 2.4-mile ocean swim, and I hate swimming. I will not swim in the ocean unless the plane goes down, and even then, it's open for discussion. Second, I've ridden my bike forty miles, and the pain was excruciating. There is no way I will ride for 112 agonizing hilly miles under the blazing sun. Lastly, I will not endure the pain associated with successfully completing the Ironman by running 26.2 miles. I cannot and do not want to do what Joan did. I just want to cross the finish line to the cheers of the crowd.

When looking for the soil to nourish your gift, it is important to figure out the difference between being Joan and being Rosalyn, between being who you are and being someone you are not.

At a recent conference, as I was leaving the podium, Jill, a young woman I'd never met came to the edge of the stage and asked if she could talk with me. She introduced herself and said she wanted to know what she could do to become "a really great speaker."

She said she was shy, hated to speak in public, and on the occasions when she had to talk in or to groups, she broke out in a rash. She'd tried public speaking classes and almost fainted when faced with having to present. She'd tried the equivalent of Toastmasters®, but could not bring herself to rise in front of her colleagues, even when she practiced the speech in her bedroom for hours the night before.

I asked Jill why she wanted to become a great speaker. Did she have friends who wouldn't listen to her? Did her boss require her to be a masterful speaker, share strategies, or deliver the state-of-the-company address in order to remain employed?

"No," she said, "but when I see people like you on stage, I want to do what you do."

I explained that speaking is my gift. The ability to talk to rooms filled with strangers wanting to be entertained and enlightened is my passion and my blessing. I told her I believe in mastering a range of skills, but I am convinced that excellence sits at the apex of diligence, strengths, and blessings. My gift was not her gift; hers was not mine.

Are you trying to be you or someone else? Who are you trying to be? What happens if you somehow become whoever that is? What happens to the person who is uniquely you when you abandon her to become someone else? The answer to this question is extremely important as you decide to do what moves your soul. Remember, the goal must be yours: for and about you.

Not sure why this is important? Get a piece of paper and something to write with. If you're right handed, use your left (if you are a lefty, use the right hand). Copy the following text in the box below using your non-dominant hand.

Women, I believe, search for fellow beings who have faced similar struggles, conveyed them in ways a reader can transform into her own life, confirmed desires the reader had hardly acknowledged - desires that now seem possible.

You can do it, but it's unnatural, uncomfortable, and a waste of the limited time you have to dedicate to your endeavor. If you love structure and order, but choose a career that is built on embracing chaos—because that is the path your older brother took—you will always feel like you are writing with the wrong hand. Working from your abilities and talents will make many things easier, more comfortable, fluid, and natural.

Have you ever wondered why your work isn't working for you? Perhaps it is because the driving force behind your choice is the desire to be someone else. I wanted to be Ironman Joan crossing the finish line. Jill wanted to be me, standing at the podium, relaxed and enjoying the moment.

Who do you want to be? Maybe the truth is that you are struggling to fit into someone else's shoes. Marcus Buckingham says, "Careers often go astray because people are competent at things they find unrewarding."[9] Your gift does not live in someone else; it lives only in you. Never settle for another's life or their gift.

The journey to excellence is arduous when you love what you're doing. If you hate getting up and facing your life, what's the point? If you have moved the debris covering your gift, the next step is finding the right soil to nurture it.

FINDING THE RIGHT SOIL

"Don't ask yourself what the world needs; ask yourself what makes you come alive. And then go and do that. Because what the world needs is people who have come alive."[10]

A seed, even a divine one, cannot survive and grow without soil. I refer to that soil as "passion." Passion is the soil that that will support, nourish, and protect your seeds of greatness. Passion is not a mental exercise. It comes from the soul. When it appears, it is forceful, powerful, and intense, not moderate or passive. Dwana Smallwood, a former Alvin Alley dancer, said, "Dance is my oxygen."[11] When you find your passion, you will know it's as essential to living as oxygen.

Passion is the positive force that makes it possible to work on the book after the kids are in bed. It gives you the strength to enroll in the ballet class at age thirty-four, an effort your mother says you're too old to attempt.

Finding your passion, your soil, is important because some seeds thrive in sandy soil, and others in clay. Some love rocky terrain; for others, black dirt is best. The right soil is needed for the right seed. How do you find the right soil? The exercise at the end of this section can help you find the right soil for you—help you find your passion.

It is important to remember that passion is what you do when you are the only one you need to please. It is what you would do even if no one cared, didn't earn you a dime, or you didn't have to impress your parents,

13

friends, or Uncle James, who said you'd never amount to anything. It's the activities that you do or would do in spite of your schedule, outstanding obligations, or external pressures.

The question women ask when I talk about passion is, "How do I know what my passion is?"

The real question is: How do I find the soil that will allow my greatness to grow? How do I identify my oxygen? Passion is doing what you love and what burns in your heart. Sounds simple, doesn't it? Yes, and I believe it is that simple. Lastly, you're wondering, "Can I make a living from a joyful life?" Read on.

LIVING ON THE ROYALTIES OF PASSION

"Every great dream begins with a dreamer. Always remember, you have within you the strength, the patience, and the passion."[12]

Perhaps you are thinking, "I have to make a living. I need to pay bills and buy shoes. I can't live off my passion. My choice is to paint and starve or continue driving this school bus."

It doesn't have to be *either* doing what you love *or* not doing what you love. There are several options. One option is to do what you love on weekends, as a part of your vacation, or in your spare time.

An artist friend of mine works four days a week at her day job and paints (when she feels like it) on day five and the weekends. Once every few years, she takes a trip with a group of women painters. That vacation allows her to do what she loves and produce more paintings to sell.

When I asked if she desired to paint full-time, her answer surprised me. She said, "I love my job, and I love painting. If I wasn't doing both, I don't think I would do either as well. Don't get me wrong; I'd love to have more time to paint and to sell lots of paintings, but I'm not sure I would be as happy if I didn't have something else to think about."

Another option is to find a way to make your passion pay all the bills. View it under the light of possibility. See the connection between the salability of what you love and the infinite marketplace. The list of examples of how passion paid the rent is endless. Dog washes, Beats® Earphones, food trucks, skate parks, and Mrs. Fields® cookies made millionaires.

To see your passion through the lens of possibility, you have to start with your gift. Imagine that from the time you were a teenager, people made fun of your need to turn chaos into order. Your closet, basement, garage, and garden all have discernible patterns. When you were six, your dolls were clothed and coiffed. Your Hot Wheels tracks were either in perfect figure eights or stacked neatly in the boxes in which they arrived. You have always loved organizing.

Thousands of people can, will, and do pay people like you to help order their lives, their taxes, their clothes, and their children's schedules. It's the passion that pays.

When people ask me how they can find their passion, I tell them to answer these three questions:

"What am I always doing?" Passion is reflected in your practices.

"What do I show up for?" Passion is reflected in your presence.

"Where do I get my fulfillment?" Passion is reflected in your rewards.

Instead of deciding that passion and pay can't have a harmonious existence, view your passion through the lens of opportunity. For example, if you answered, "shopping" to all of the above questions, maybe there's a way for you to do what you love and are blessed to do and pay the rent. One man turned his love of shopping into a paycheck.

I met Jason at a gala in Los Angeles. I love stylish clothing, and he looked like he just stepped off the red carpet at a Hollywood premiere. We were seated at the same table, and we began to talk. When I asked what he did, he said he was a personal shopper for a wealthy woman. He beamed as he shared that his job was to shop with and for her and, as he said, "Make sure she looked and felt beautiful." He traveled around the world with her, attended interesting events, and fulfilled his dream of buying beautiful and expensive things. I am positive that his is not the only available client.

Maybe you will need more than one venue for your passion. Lori and I crossed paths many years ago, when I was looking for someone to sing at my wedding. Several people recommended her, and when I heard her, I understood why she came so highly recommended.

Lori loves music. It is her calling and her profession. She has loved music as far back as she can remember. To support herself and her passion, she teaches at the arts high school. It pays the rent and feeds her soul. She also has an A-list of private music students and performs at notable events.

Her public and private students love her because her passion for music shows in every lesson. She plays and sings at events large and small, and always with the same extraordinary spirit and dedication. Her music pays the bills, keeps her body alive, and provides her the "oxygen"[13] she needs to breath.

Whether your passion becomes a moneymaker or remains your weekend pleasure is up to you. You actually can have your cake and eat it, too. Don't we all want that? Many women have found ways to do what they love. I want to introduce you to three of them. They have similar and yet different stories of how they live their passion.

Joi Gordon – Passionate Leader

Is it possible to be passionate and change the world at the same time? Can your gift take you around the world and allow you to better the lives of hundreds of thousands of women, their families, and their communities? Yes. It can. Of all the people I met while working for MTV Networks in New York City, Joi Gordon remains not only one of my sheroes,[14] but also an example of the power of living your passion every day with energy, determination, and heart, in the process changing the world.

Joi Gordon CEO, Dress for Success, was raised in a family rich in tradition, achievement, and social responsibility. She graduated from the University of Oklahoma, College of Law, and was on the road to financial prosperity and career achievement. She had everything except a love for her work. Although putting people in prison wasn't her dream job, it paid the bills and her school loans. After watching a TV show about Dress for Success, she decided to check it out. Something about the organization and the women it served drew her in. She found herself working in the basement of a run-down NY building, not as a pro bono attorney, but as a volunteer helping women put their wardrobes and lives back together. She grew from that to CEO.

She contacted me, and we met for lunch. She wanted me to join the Worldwide Board of Dress for Success, and I said, "Yes." What I remember most about the conversation was her love of the organization. It was contagious.

Today, her extraordinary negotiating and networking skills make her successful, and her passion makes her legendary. She is an ardent champion, determined to find innovative and inspired ways to help women achieve financial, spiritual, and economic self-sufficiency.

I asked Joi why she does this year after year and she said, "I live the most blessed and satisfying life I could ever imagine. Every day, I work with women I love. It's not the title or the compliments, the awards or being on the cover of a magazine that drives me. It's seeing a woman go from sadness and desperation to feeling powerful and whole."

Joi Gordon's spirit infects everyone who meets her. She brings women from the most horrific circumstances to the consciousness of the corporate elite. How? She breathes life into the description of a woman's story. It's her laugh as she tells the story of giving up her shoes so a client who needed them could go to her interview, or the way she can make you hear the sound of her heart breaking when she talks of the pain on the face of a woman as she struggles, fails, and gets up and tries again.

Her passion for the organization and her love for the women it serves is alive and compelling. Her love for life and her work is a fire that warms anyone who stands near her. Think you can't live a passionate life? Think again.

Alison – Passionate Entrepreneur

It is not always easy to live a passionate life. Maybe you have failed, and you are afraid to try again. Perhaps you know what makes you happy, but you wonder if it is worth the effort, the possibility of another failure, or the uphill battle that often comes with being fully alive. What motivates us can be the result of many things. Media mogul Oprah Winfrey said, "Where there is no struggle, there is no strength."[15]

Some of us are driven by a struggle that surrounds the seed of greatness and pushes it through the soil and into the light. That is what I saw when I met Alison Rhodes more than a decade ago. Driven by a mountain-sized passion for creating safe practices and protected spaces for parents and children, Alison Rhodes founded Peek-A-Boo Baby Proofing, Inc. She started this business to honor her first child, Conner, who succumbed to sudden infant death syndrome (SIDS). She found that helping families allowed her to unite her passion and her business savvy and created a million-dollar business, in which doing good and doing well came together.

By the time we met, she had been featured on *ABC World News Tonight*, *Court TV*, Oxygen's *The Gayle King Show*, PBS' *Keeping Kids Healthy*, and in publications and websites including *American Baby Magazine*, Parenting.com, SheKnows.com, and *Expectant Mother*, but the fame and the money were not what drove her. She was intriguing and upbeat, despite the motivation for her work. When Alison and I sat down and shared life stories, I knew immediately that notoriety did not move her; it was doing work that satisfied her deeper longing—a fire in her heart.

Alison was extremely successful by all measures, but that's what living the passionate life is. It is knowing that what you do is what you would do, whether it made you rich or just barely paid the rent. When I asked what she would do if she were not doing this, she did not hesitate.

"This is it. Other than my family, nothing else means as much to me. It's my life's work."

An update from Allison's website:

My next son is born with intellectual and developmental disabilities. My dad develops Alzheimer's and suffers a stroke and I officially became a member of the sandwich generation … [and] my husband of two years was diagnosed with Progressive Multiple Sclerosis.

So here I am today – a woman who has been thrown a bunch of curveballs in life – death, disability, debt and divorce – but still manages to be grateful, happy and passionate about everything I do. My platform (or maybe soapbox) has evolved from child safety to motivating women to live a life of health, wellness and happiness as they care for their family. In 2014 I'll be doing presentations for women on how to 'find themselves' again – the woman they were and can be before they were caring for everyone in their lives but themselves.[16]

Passion is a choice. Choose "yes."

Stacy – Passionate Youth

Can you recognize and embrace your gift when you're seventeen, or is pursuing your joy reserved for people who can legally purchase wine?

As I talked with people about passion, the elusive catalyst, I found that one way to get them in touch with the thing that moved their soul was to ask them what they loved to do when they were younger. It would make sense, then, that there are young women whom if asked, could articulate what they are passionate about.

Many of us are closer to our passions when we are young, and they become less available to us as we age. Maybe that is because when a young woman expresses her passion to her parents, teachers, and girlfriends, they actively or passively discourage her. Perhaps they want to protect her from the pain and disappointment of failure. Possibly, they are worried that they will be required to provide time, money, or transportation. Whatever the reason, our youthful vision of our passion fades. This often leads to living an ordinary life when we could just as easily aspire to be extraordinary. The following story of achieving greatness is for all of our daughters, nieces, and granddaughters, the next generation of women who will follow their passion.

I was having sushi one evening when I met a mother, father, and their seventeen-year-old daughter, Stacy. Stacy not only longed to travel to Japan, she had a plan. Her parents were not sure what triggered this intense desire, but they were certain that this was Stacy's true and unwavering passion—to travel to and possibly live in Japan. This was an African-American family. If they said she wanted to visit South Africa, it would have more easily fit my picture, but it wasn't Cape Town or Senegal; it was Tokyo and Osaka, Japan.

Stacy reminded me of Maya Angelou's quote, "I love to see a young girl go out and grab the world by the lapels."[17] To finance the trip of her dreams, Stacy convinced her mother to match any monies she earned, and this spunky young woman worked two part-time jobs, much to her mother's amazement and chagrin. She joked, "This is going to cost me millions. And she's thinking about getting a third job!"

Here was a woman-child who identified her Personal Legend,[18] her goal, something that ignited her passion and gave her the courage to

22

follow it. Stacy had become fluent in Japanese. She read articles, books, and searched the Internet for new and necessary information. She was constantly learning about the culture. While we had dinner, she was conversing in Japanese with the staff at the sushi bar and trying to absorb as much knowledge as possible. Everyone she encountered knew to what she aspired. She gathered support from her family, friends, and anyone who would listen.

Her desires were clear. She wanted to travel to Japan after graduating from high school. She knew how much it would cost and had a schedule to earn it. Her father said that no matter where they went, she talked with people about Japan, hoping to learn something or establish contacts she could call when she arrived. There was no doubt that in the near future she would be sending her parents postcards from Tokyo.

With any luck, you're starting to see that your discontent may not be your boring job, the dieting merry-go-round, or the person snoring on the couch next to you, who you now refer to as "the idiot." What's really wrong? You're not doing something that waters and feeds your passion and your soul.

What Joi, Alison, and Stacy found was a way to live a passionate life. From law school to Japan, with pain and determination, these three passionate women, although different in many ways, discovered and pursued their passions. If these three women are right, and I think they are, the only thing that can bring real joy—lasting and satisfying happiness, even in difficult times—is to find your seeds of greatness and the soil that will allow it to bear fruit.

LIVING PASSIONATELY

EXERCISE #1

Choose three to five people who know you and want you to find your voice. Explain to each person that you hope to uncover and understand your divine gift, or at least a life that makes you smile. Sit down with each person. Try not to judge, influence, or control their answers. Encourage them to say what is true and not what they think you want to hear. Then listen, receive, and record their answers to these three questions:

1. What do you think I love to do? (Ex: read, talk, paint, network, cook, play, act)

2. What do you think is my major motivator, the thing that gets me up in the morning? (Ex: altruism, social responsibility, fame, money, learning, creating, entertaining, service)

3. In order for me to get to a place where I can do what I love, what are the biggest areas and opportunities for improvement? What do I need to work on first, second, third?

LIVE PASSIONATELY

EXERCISE #2

Find some relaxed and uninterrupted time. Answer these three questions. Don't judge or censure yourself.

1) What would I do for free, with no pay? (Ex: write children's books, cook, etc.)

2) What have I enjoyed doing since I was young? (Ex: collecting, organizing, painting, etc.)

3) What do I do that my friends and colleagues think I'm good at? (Ex: decorate my home, teach kids to surf, help people deal with their computer problems, etc.)

LIVE PASSIONATELY

EXERCISE #3

Dig a little deeper. Answer these questions with an example to support your answer.

Do I prefer to work alone or with a group?

Do I like to be in front of the camera or behind the scenes?

How do I feel about financial instability?

Do I work better with structure or prefer to rely on my wits? Do I prefer to make it up as I go along or to have a plan?

Am I better at addressing conflict or negotiating a price?

What do I see first—the big picture or the details?

Do I prefer working with inanimate objects like furniture, or do I enjoy working with animals, children, or adults?

LIVE PASSIONATELY

EXERCISE #4

Now let's identify your strengths. This is your assessment, although you can ask others to provide feedback. Mark seven words that you feel describe your strengths and then rank them 1 through 7, 7 being the highest. You can add one or two others, if you choose, but pick the seven that most describe your strengths.

	Select	Rank
Confident		
Expressive		
Goal oriented		
Decisive		
Creative		
Risk taker		
Organized		
Hard worker		
Supportive		
Accountable		
Professional		
Good listener		
Positive attitude		

LIVE PASSIONATELY

EXERCISE #5

Read and review the answers in these four exercises. Study your answers. Record the common threads between all of these exercises.

Using your answer to the above question, complete these three sentences.

1) If I had all the money I needed, I would

2) It's clear that I would like to

3) I'm not sure yet, but I think I would like to: (Guess. There is no penalty, and you cannot be "wrong.")

LIVE PASSIONATELY

THINGS TO REMEMBER

- The divinity places seeds of greatness in all of us.

- Passion is the soil that nourishes your seeds of greatness.

- You can live off the royalties of your passion.

- Passion is reflected in your practices. "What am I always doing?"

- Passion is reflected in your presence. "What do I show up for?"

- Passion is reflected in your rewards. "Where do I get my fulfillment?"

- Passion is not a thing. It is a relationship between your heart and your hands.

- Connect your passion and the global marketplace.

CHAPTER 2

COURAGE IS KEY

"There are people who put their dreams in a little box and say, 'Yes, I've got dreams, of course I've got dreams.' Then they put the box away and bring it out once in a while to look in it, and yep, they're still there. It takes an uncommon amount of guts to put your dreams on the line to hold them up and say, 'How good or how bad am I?' That's where courage comes in."

—Erma Bombeck

It's Time for Bravery

"Courage is the most important of all the virtues, because without courage you can't practice any other virtue consistently. You can practice any virtue erratically, but nothing consistently without courage."[9]

What did Joi Gordon, Alison Rhodes, and Stacy (see "Living on the Royalties of Passion") all have in common? They had the courage to walk *toward* their dreams.

Passion comes alive when you put on your big girl pants and take the first steps toward your dream, when you decide to bring water (courage) to the soil (passion). Courage enables you to go from sitting on the couch, eating fried chicken and cookie dough while watching the newest *Better Butt* exercise video to actually living your dream of an active and healthy life.

You know what I'm talking about. You look in the mirror and see the woman you are and not the one you want to be. Your clothes don't fit. You've blamed it on PMS, PMD, menopause, having children, lack of exercise, white-flour addiction, and your lazy spouse. Or maybe you opened your checkbook and realized that for the twelfth straight year, you have no money. You can barely pay the bills. There's no vacation fund, Christmas club, college savings account for you or the kids, and if the car gets a flat, you'll need to declare bankruptcy.

A beautiful woman-friend and colleague, Candi Castleberry Singleton, shared the following with me, and I've shared it with many others. This is where we begin.

Today is all we have.

Yesterday is gone and nothing can bring it back.

Tomorrow is only a dream.

Make sure that when today is over, you have done all that you can to live a full, courageous, and passionate life.

For today is all you have.

Yesterday is gone, and nothing can bring it back.

Tomorrow is only a dream.[20]

Maybe your voyage begins at your twenty-fifth high school reunion. Marsha, who sat next to you in most of your classes, enters the room to a flurry of whispers. You remember her as someone who wasn't that smart or pretty, so why all the fuss? Everyone at the table knows the answer.

Marsha is on the cover of *Successful Business Women* magazine. She recently sold her third company for twenty-two million dollars, and at age 43 is taking a six-month, around-the-world tour before retiring in Belize. As you take it all in, you hear a small voice in your head whisper, "That's what I want, but I'm not sure where to begin."

Today you are ready to take that first step. You're no longer satisfied with the paycheck, your workplace has become stale, and the seventy-three-minute commute is unbearable. On your lunch break, you think about an idea that's been rattling around your head for years. It is your dream to be an entrepreneur. You smile. You're open to the possibility. It would be nice to do something different, to step out of the comfortable but uninspired grind, and challenge yourself.

"I'm not afraid of failing, and I'm smart," you say to your compact mirror as you put the finishing touches on your lipstick and check your teeth for salad remnants. You smile. You're all set.

Suddenly, staring back at you in the mirror is your mother. "You can't leave your job. You don't have anything to fall back on. And you have obligations."

Your older sister yells in your ear, "Hey, stop dreaming!"

You turn away and notice a newspaper on the table behind you. There, in black and white, is story after story about businesses that are closing, increasing corporate layoffs, and a job market that's less welcoming of women your age.

"Maybe I should call a friend who's an entrepreneur and ask her what she thinks," you say to the people ignoring you at the other tables. In your heart, you know you don't need more advice.

Fortunately, today, something is different. You can feel it taking root. You know you're ready, and it doesn't matter what you hear. You've decided that staying in your current job and on your safe but uninteresting career path is more painful than risking failure. You have chosen to move forward and follow your heart. You're not going to settle for headlines or advice. You close the compact, tell your sister to shut up, and throw the newspaper into the recycling bin. The guy it belonged to says something, but you ignore him and all the other distractions.

It may difficult and uncomfortable to let go of the familiar but monotonous life you're leading and follow your dreams and aspirations, but you are ready. You've found a clean stream with enough water (courage) to nourish the soil (passion), and you're ready to add it to your dreams. Courage, like water, may be difficult to find or need to be brought from far away. But it is important to remember that courage separates the seeds that take root from those that are merely tossed onto the ground. Sometimes courage is a light sprinkling; other times, it is a monsoon. You may have to dance for it, dig deep wells, or carry it across the dessert.

From the sky, the well, or melting mountain snow, water allows the seed to expand, grow, and mature. Without courage (water), the seed eventually dries up and disintegrates into would-haves and could-haves. Without the right amount of water, the seed will not be able to put deep roots into the soil to withstand the changing seasons or survive the raging windstorms and grow strong.

For some of you, finding water for the soil is as simple as submitting the proposal you tucked away in the folder labeled "Tomorrow," but for others, the next step is much harder and more perilous. It's time find the water in the desert, the courage buried deep in uncertainties, and confront your fears.

KNOW THYSELF

ESTHER'S STORY

"You are the designer of your destiny. You are the author of your story."[21]

While living in Manhattan, New York, I met Esther, one of six homeless African-Americans I saw three or four times a week on my 5:30 a.m. runs. She called me "the granola lady," because on my runs through Central Park, I handed out granola bars—my way of honoring my mother, who taught me that giving should be a daily act, not an annual event.

I often stopped to talk to the women and men who considered the park their home. It was a great excuse to catch my breath, and I truly enjoyed the company of the people who shared their lives without pretenses or agendas. On this particular morning, Esther and I talked longer than usual. My assignment was ending, and as I prepared to return to California, I was aware that I would miss this chapter in my life.

We talked about how much I longed for my home. (I lived in a beautiful apartment in New York City, but it wasn't *home*.) I asked her, "What do you wish for? What do you dream of having?" I expected her to wax nostalgic about a small house with a garden and a front porch. Isn't it true we give our wishes to others and believe they will gratefully accept them?

She said, "I have it. I am free. Every day when I wake up, I am free. I spent almost thirty years living in a wheelchair, unable to leave my house. I swore that if I ever got out of that chair, I'd never be confined to anything again."

I will never forget the joy in her face as she talked about being unbound (my word). Being free (her word) was her dream come true. It moved her heart, defined how she lived her life, and clearly indicated what she was willing to sacrifice.

A nice house with a roof, doors, and windows might represent the brass ring for some, but it represented a very different picture for her. The roof and doors symbolized imprisonment, not the American Dream. When I share this story, often the listener says, "Yes, but someday she'll change her mind and want to have a normal life." Translation: she'll want what I want. But her passion and her dream felt as reasonable to me as my own.

Esther was clearly happy with her choices. It takes an enormous amount of bravado to live on the streets of New York. Esther had the courage to follow her heart and her dream. When you wonder if you can live the life of your choosing, remember Esther, who followed her heart from bound to free.

DON'T LET FEAR WIN

"Start where you are. Use what you have. Do what you can."[22]

Now that you've decided to move forward, you start to feel nauseous. You let fear lead you to believe that you will never have a career that satisfies you, and that you'll end up working a job that requires you to wear a hairnet. Perhaps as you think about what you want, you start to imagine every possible negative outcome, and like Fire Marshall Bill on *In Living Color*,[23] you turn a minor mistake into a disaster.

You listen to the voice in your head that says, "You want to own a profitable consulting business? There'll be a recession. Every potential client will be reducing staff and unable to afford your services. Your home office computer will crash, and all of your data files will be irretrievably lost, and of course, you'll slip on a wet floor, which will result in permanent memory loss."

You place the most unreasonable obstacles in your path, create a negative story line, fill in the details with great care, develop all of the characters, and write the plot that has your life going down the tubes.

Here is another way to go.

Six friends came together in search of their dream, to build a strong, vibrant, and financially secure business. They formed IN-Genius Consulting and built their reputation for innovative solutions with a growing client base. The small but dedicated team talked about how crucial it was to turn strangers into customers. They recognized the importance of contacts to a fledgling organization.

One day, fortune smiled on them. They received an invitation to attend a black-tie event at the mayor's residence. This was a chance to network with some the most influential people on their "wish list."

As they read the invitation, fear whispers, "Leslie, it's black tie you idiot, and none of you have or can afford to buy proper clothes."

"Kelly, the people at this event will be elitist snobs. By the time the appetizers arrive, they'll be making fun of you, pointing, and laughing."

"Maria, you won't make any contacts, and you'll get drunk, insult the host, and spill red wine on the mayor's white shirt."

If they gave into their fears of being embarrassed, feeling like outsiders, or behaving like idiots, the IN-Genius team would miss an opportunity for their growing business. One of the team members, Talia, heard her voice of courage.

She gathered the team and said, "If you don't have clothes, borrow a dark suit from your father, a black dress from your sister, and shoes from your niece. If we call enough friends, someone will help. The people who love us want us to succeed. The six of us are already a group, so we won't be alone or lonely."

The newest team member, Janice, chimed in, "Let's make a pact that if anyone sees a team member in trouble or about to get into trouble, they will say the code word "junket," and we will leave, stop drinking, or take her skirt out of her underwear."

Would the night work out perfectly? Not likely. Would it be a disaster? No, I assure you it would not.

The next step is harder and more perilous. It's time find the water in the desert; the courage buried deep in uncertainties, and confront your fears.

TALK TO YOUR FEARS

"Our deepest fear is not that we are inadequate. Our deepest fear is that we are powerful beyond measure. It is our Light, not our Darkness, that most frightens us."[24]

Start by declaring what you want in your life. You're tired of watching reruns of *How I Met Your Mother*[25] and sharing "interesting animal pairs" on your Facebook page. You want to find someone who loves and respects you, shares your values, and cares about your family and friends. Often, when you ask the Universe for help, it sends you a present. Do you have the courage to do what is necessary to receive it?

Here's how the gift might appear. Your friend Tyron is hosting a small, intimate dinner party. It is the perfect opportunity to meet new friends. Your fear of rejection gathers steam from your fear of intimacy, and together they convince you that, "There's no one out there worth meeting because if they are wonderful, they already have someone special."

Stop the Conversation in Your Head

Say aloud, "I don't have someone, and I am wonderful." (In Chapter 11, we will discuss the importance of the words that follow "I am.") It's unlikely that in a country of at least a billion people, you're the only one who's single and wonderful.

Dread whispers, "You're not ready. You haven't lost enough weight, and you need to have a face, chin, and butt lift. Your hair's not perfect, and you need to whiten your teeth."

Stop the Conversation in Your Head

Listen, girlfriend, you will never be perfect, and because that's the truth, if you want to test the waters, you will just have to go as you are today. You can change your outsides, but that is not the problem. It is that voice on the inside. Your chin, face, butt, and every other part is yours! Learn to love them now; change them later.

Perhaps your little voice says, "It's too cold, hot, rainy, or dry to go out. Your hair, makeup, or nail polish will be ruined." Well, wear a coat, take a comb, or put on gloves. If you live in Alaska or Arizona, you still need love.

Fear does not leave quietly. It shouts in your ear, "There's a great rerun of *Basic Instinct*[26] on TV tonight. Remember what happened to Michael Douglas when he went out?" You can stop worrying. You're not Michael Douglas or Sharon Stone. The key to reaching your goal is matching your words to your walk (the second Key in Chapter 4). Your behaviors tell everyone what is important and what you believe.

Does it really matter if you don't find your true love tonight? No, it's practice. You're working on your three-minute elevator speech, the one that tells people who you are and why they want to know you. You're developing stories that can be used later in the game. You're sharpening the saw.[27] Every person you meet at this party is a potential advocate and supporter. The very action of going out, talking with, and listening to strangers builds your confidence and reinforces positive feelings.

Courage is defined as "the state or quality of mind or spirit that enables one to face fear...with self-possession and resolution."[28] Stop telling yourself why you can't, won't, or shouldn't. Sometimes what you stop doing is more important than what you start doing.

IF IT'S ABUSIVE, GET OUT

"You've got to know when to hold them, know when to fold them, know when to walk away, know when to run."[29]

I am convinced that it may be more courageous to run away than stay. I am convinced that it is almost impossible to grow into whom God meant you to be when you wake up every day scared and anxious. I learned this lesson the hard way. I don't wonder how I got here, but I am trying to remember why I couldn't leave before we came to this day. Nothing in this story has been changed; the innocent do not need to be protected.

I am standing in the living room. Lee has a can of gasoline and a BIC® lighter. She is drunk, angry, screaming, and threatening to set herself and everything around her on fire. That includes our house (her house), her beloved and evil Siamese cat, and me.

She has long, dark lashes that frame golden irises the color of cat's eyes. They're not hazel or light brown, but gold, like the color inside the marbles I played with when I was nine. It was the first thing I noticed about her. The second thing I noted was that she could be mean. When she was drinking, which was five out of seven days a week, she was what my mother called a "nasty drunk." I knew the difference because my grandfather was a "sweet drunk." When my grandfather drank, he played the piano and serenaded anyone who would listen. When Lee drank, she broke things, destroyed expensive furniture, and raged against anyone who loved her.

Many of us loved her. Bright, competent, successful women who could have loved and been loved by many others were drawn together to love Lee. The strange thing was that she never tricked any of us. Within two days of knowing her, you experienced the demons—the drinking, shouting, fighting, and uncontrollable temper. At the same time, Lee had something that made her lovable and likable to strangers. The owner of the hardware store, waiters at our favorite restaurant, and drag queens at the gay bar were glad to see her. They treated her like family. At the bar and restaurant, they had her favorite drink ready by the time we sat down.

Three or ten drinks into the night she would smash a glass against a wall or turn over chairs as she stumbled to the bathroom. They'd bring us the check and tell her she'd had enough and it was time to leave. And she would, without drama or incident. The next week, or a month later, they welcomed her back as if nothing had happened. But once we reached the street, her rage turned to me, or anyone who loved her and had accompanied her that night. She would start a physical fight. This was before anti-domestic violence campaigns, and because it was between two women, it was never reported.

We punched each other. She'd slap me, and I would push her. I would grab her wrist and twist it until she released the car keys. I knew she was not capable of driving, but it took every ounce of strength to take the keys from her. Then I had to try to get her into the car. She would walk in the middle of the street, narrowly avoiding oncoming traffic. She would throw trashcans or anything not tied or chained down.

When she got into the car, (she had bad ankles and even inebriated she couldn't walk more than a few blocks) she would scratch, punch, and hit me. I hit back. A lifetime and fifteen minutes later, when we arrived at the house, she would stagger up the stairs, pour a drink, and continue to kill brain cells. Most of the time, I could tell when her memory shut down—the blackout. I could do anything I wanted to her, and she would not remember. Nor would she remember anything she'd done to me or anyone else. Sometimes the evidence from the previous night was the welt on the side of my face or the scratches on my arm. More often, the turned-over furniture, broken glass, or torn curtains on the floor told the story.

I stayed with her for four years. Every few days, I'd promise myself to leave her, find an apartment, and become a normal twenty-something, but like many of you I vacillated. I couldn't leave, but I couldn't stay. I didn't leave until the night of the gasoline.

I remember wondering when she filled up the gas can. As she stood in the middle of the room, I noticed the look in her eyes that meant she was incapable of rational thought. She talked about me leaving her. She said she would rather burn down the house and everything in it than live in it without me. She asked me if I thought she would do it, and I said, "Yes, I'm sure you can."

"If you walk out that door," she screamed, "I'm going to burn down this fuckin house."

She had the can in one hand and the lighter in the other. At that moment, my worry that she might kill herself if I left meant less than the reality that she was willing to set us both on fire. The next day, when (if) I awoke in the burn unit, she'd be sorry or dead.

American author, feminist, and social activist Bell Hooks said, "All too often women believe it is a sign of commitment, an expression of love, to endure unkindness or cruelty, to forgive and forget. In actuality, when we love rightly we know that the healthy, loving response to cruelty and abuse is putting ourselves out of harm's way."[30] I moved out of harm's way and into the YWCA. I was a twenty-four-year-old middle-class Black woman in the company of twenty or thirty women with similarly sad tales, but I was alive, and with that came the chance to take the steps that began my journey of a thousand miles.

Maybe what stands between you and joy is the thought that it's too late for you. You've done too many stupid things, abused your body and soul, and now it's too late to heal. Don't let fear win! When I say it is never too late, I speak as a woman who's been inside the asylum and now walks the street—free and blessed.

Is it time for *you* to get out of harm's way and start over? Yes! Find the courage your passion needs in order to survive and thrive. Remember, without water, the plant will never flower.

CONFRONT THE SHAME

"We can only love others as much as we love ourselves."[31]

This section may be difficult to read. I talk about things that are often buried under the heading of "don't tell people your business." I worry "people won't like me when they know who I really am," but I hope that when you read my words, when you hear me telling my truth, that you will be able to do the same. It is liberating, and a little scary, to tell you my *real* stories—the good, the bad, the ugly, and the extraordinary.

While working on the final edit of *Passion, Courage, and Faith*, a family member called to tell me that my nephew, who had been spiraling out of control for several months, had been placed on a 24-hour, involuntary psychiatric hold. As I write these words I can hear my deceased mother and every living family member telling me that it is not ok to share this family secret. The only concession I made was to get his permission to share this.

At the same time this was occurring, I was reading scholar, author, and shame resilience expert Brené Brown's *The Gifts of Imperfection: Let Go of Who You Think You're Supposed to Be and Embrace Who You Are* and former TV host and author Iyana Vanzant's *Peace from Broken Pieces: How to Get Through What You're Going Through*.

I needed to hear their messages - for myself and for my nephew. Both authors were telling me that shame lives behind the curtain of civility.

That it grows when we deny it and not when we name it. Shame, they wrote, conceals itself in the lying I'd been brought up to believe was the only way to live. Not the "Did you lock the door? Yes, I did" kind of lie. I'm talking about the lies that damaged my soul. The mandatory pretending that everything inside the home looked like everything outside—at church, school, and family events—loving, calm, and respectful.

In truth, there was constant anger, shouting, violence, and smoldering hatred. The danger of physical harm was always present. Everyone except me had loaded guns in their cars, closets, and dresser drawers. It seems like I was always moving from terror fueled by my fear that my parents would kill one another to the equally horrifying dread that they wouldn't, and I would have to live in this hell forever. The worst part was never being able to talk with anyone about it.

Fear grew into shame—embarrassed by my thoughts, ashamed of my dread and my fear. Shame led me to seek relief in unhealthy and dangerous behaviors. Although it was my way of saying, "F— you" to the world, specifically my parents, it was extremely destructive. I grew up ashamed of my body, so I trashed it. I refused to feed it (today it's called an "eating disorder"), and at age twelve, I let sixteen-year-old boys use my body. At thirteen, I staggered into my parent's mega-Memorial Day barbecue so drunk I almost died of alcohol poisoning.

As I grew, so did my disgrace. At seventeen, I started visiting porn theaters, where I allowed strangers to cross bounds of decency. I let people who were completely unworthy use my body. I drank, took handfuls of pills, smoked cigarettes and pot, and engaged in every unhealthy behavior you can imagine.

For some of you, shame led to promiscuity, alcoholism, abusive relationships, or drug abuse. For me, it was all of these and more. Those behaviors, innocent at first, but ultimately horrifying, built my shame wall brick by painful brick. This wall of shame surrounded me, separating me from love and comfort.

My humiliation as the drug-abusing, sexualized twelve-year-old who became a promiscuous woman haunted me until I realized that we deal with life with the tools we have. If I'd had other tools, I would have used them. I didn't, and neither did you.

It took me years of therapy and a commitment to looking at this every day to take the wall apart. I examined individual bricks, naming them and honoring that they are not who I am, but what my battered spirit did to mask and quiet the raging child. This is how I knew my nephew was suffering from profound shame. Shame that with everything that he'd been given—caring parents, great family life, private schools, and all the trappings of happiness, he hadn't become the successful young man everyone thought he should be. It was a shame that he could only quiet by getting high. When that didn't still the demons, he lashed out at the people he loved and who loved him. In nineteen years, it grew from smoking a little pot to talk of ending his life.

Everyone thought my nephew's behaviors originated in anger, but I knew what the physical manifestations of shame felt like—the burning in my cheeks, the tightness in my throat, and the shallow breathing. I also recognized using screaming tirades to mask humiliation. I tell you this because unexamined feelings of shame can and likely will blow up at the most inopportune times and in ways that exacerbate your degradation. Here's how it happened to my dear mentee, "Cassandra."

Cassandra taught me two things: first, that the combination of blame and shame is toxic, and second, not every story has a happy ending.

Being courageous when you come from a life that feels barren and filled with jagged rocks isn't easy. Cassandra had conquered drug addition, overcome homelessness, and found work that valued her skills and praised her ethics and resilient spirit. She was on a path toward a better life. During one of our mentoring sessions, she shared her desire to lose weight and become healthy and to heal the damage years of abuse had inflicted on her body.

Weight loss represented the area of her life that connected her past and future. When she was an addict, her drug activities kept her mind off eating, so she didn't gain weight. After four years clean and sober, her body was returning to its metabolic balance, and weight gain was a part of the process.

When her mother died the twins, *shame* and *blame*, took over her life. Cassandra carried a mountain of shame for what her drug addiction forced her to do—steal, lie, and cheat the people she loved, including her mother. She blamed herself for her mother losing the house she worked years to buy. Her mom had mortgaged her precious home to help pay Cassandra's legal bills. Every day, Cassandra felt the horrible weight of the twins.

After her mother passed away, the weight she gained in recovery increased. Her mom was the one person she'd gone to when she was afraid or faced with difficult choices and decisions. Her mother had supported her journey from addiction to sobriety. Cassandra found herself ankle deep in the quicksand of her past. Ashamed of the person she had been and not able to embrace the person she had become, she filled the void of her unresolved pain with bagels, chocolate, and ice cream. She said that eating sugary, high-calorie donuts was soothing. I knew it was her way of avoiding pain, uncertainty, and feelings of loss.

As she put on weight, she felt increasingly out of control and angry with herself. She was embarrassed by how she looked and ashamed of the message it sent to friends and others. She alternately acknowledged that she was the reason for her weight gain and blamed her new job that required her (at her request) to work overtime. That was her past holding on.

When I asked what she was doing to move closer to her goal to be healthy and have control over what she ate and how she looked, I heard, "I'm going to do something about it tomorrow."

She insisted that she didn't have time to exercise on a regular basis, but she was going to get started on a serious program "tomorrow." Every conversation began with what she was going to do, starting tomorrow, when she had a magical week with unlimited free time, and not what she did yesterday or today. The toxic twins—blame and shame—were holding Cassandra hostage. She could not move forward until she gained the courage to face her past and future.

I wish this story ended happily. It didn't. Cassandra gave in to the inner voices that recounted all of her failures and none of her successes. She lost her job and returned to the life she knew best: poverty, unemployment, and pain.

My hope for my nephew, my friend Cassandra, and you is that it doesn't take you fifty years to face the ways shame has shaped your life.

Shame hides in our secrets. Part of growing stronger is unlocking the box that holds the years of secrets. Get the help that will allow you to look at your past and realize that those events are also the things that brought you to where you are today, and that's not all bad.

Now pick up that watering can and get moving.

GROWING STRONGER

"She wasn't tracking down her [mother] to learn more about [her]. She was tracking [her] down to learn more about herself."[32]

In 1986, through an odd turn of circumstances, I learned that when I was two, Charles and Katherine Smith adopted me. My birth certificate and all formal records had been altered. I was not biologically related to anyone I'd known for the last thirty-four years. Although it was shocking, it didn't come as a complete surprise. There were clues; pictures I should have been in but wasn't, family rituals that took place years after they should have, and a sense that people knew things I didn't.

Yes, I'd always suspected it, but most of us at some point believe that the people sitting around the dinner table—who claim to be our parents and siblings—can't be our real family: they're just too crazy, too strange, not smart enough, too country, or too something. But although I suspected it, the reality was a jolt. I had a million questions. Who was I? What was my story? Who were my biological parents? Were there medical issues that I needed to know about? (Years later, the cancer answered this question.) Had I been intimate with a close blood relative? Don't laugh. "You and your boyfriend look like you could be brother and sister" took on new meaning.

I wanted to find the people who could answer these questions, my birth family. I quickly learned that this would be a major test because it meant facing real and imagined demons, including the adoption processes of 1950, and most importantly, my mother, Katherine. My mother, whose love and respect was the basis for much of my success, was extremely pained by my need to find what she called my "real mother."

Fear, ambiguity, uncertainty, and an antiquated paper trail stood between and me the answers to very important questions. As much as I wanted the answers, I was quietly terrified of them. It's the can-of-worms dilemma: once you've opened it, there's no way to close it and pretend you haven't seen the dirt move. Fear whispered, "What if your birthmother is on death row?" Some of you laugh or scoff, but there *are* women on death row. Some of these women are mothers, and one of them could have been mine.

You might wonder why I did not make my imaginary birth mother someone beautiful, rich, and famous, like Lena Horne? (If you're asking, "Who is she?" — think Beyoncé in about fifty years - and if you don't know who Beyoncé is "Welcome to Earth"). Fear made it easier to believe that I was more likely the product of a woman whose life went badly than one whose story was a Lifetime® TV original.

In the evening, when everything was quiet, fear told me, "If your birth mother is on death row or some other place of desperation and despair, you will be obligated to do whatever it takes to help her. That may mean mortgaging your home to mount a legal defense or put her into rehab, building a space for her in your house, or taking care of her in her failing health."

Fear didn't stop there. It offered the possibility that Katherine, the only mother I'd known, might never speak to me again. Or worse, that she'd look at me with the deep sadness of one who has been irreparably damaged by an ungrateful daughter. She and my father gave me a family, took care of me when I was sick, fought for me when I rebelled, and sent me into the world with skills and pride.

Family friends rallied around her. My godmother called to tell me that no good could come from my search. My aunts told me that what I was doing would kill my mother. Fortunately, I knew better than that. My mom caused angina in others and had survived every disease known to womankind, but it *would* break her heart.

If that wasn't enough, I was filled with worry, panic, and dread that my birthmother would reject me. I would find out who she was, and when I contacted her, she would deny any connection. She would say, "I never put a daughter up for adoption, and don't ever call me again." This rejection would not be based on circumstances. This time, it would be personal.

Maybe I would never find her. All avenues would lead to dead ends. My intelligence, resources, creativity, and ingenuity would be useless in the face of the bureaucracy of the adoption machine and a records system that was almost forty years old.

With all of this uncertainty, dread, and fright, I dug deep for a well that held the water I needed and found my courage. I turned over every stone. Each time someone told me "no" or "you can't," I dug deeper for water. At every dead end and brick wall, I searched for a glimmer of light and another way in or out. When I became too frightened to continue, I talked with friends who gave me the encouragement I needed to continue. They told me that I was strong enough to find the answers. How it turned out is another book for another time. For me, the story is about confronting my fears, both real and imagined. Every time we face our fears, stare them down, and outlast or outlive them, we grow exponentially stronger.

COURAGE

EXERCISE #1

What do I want to do?_____ (Refer to Passion Exercise #4)

What are your phobias (fears)? Be creative with the names. For example:

Stupidaphobia – fear of looking stupid

Rejectaphobia – fear of being rejected by people you want to respect you

Successphobia – fear of succeeding beyond your wildest dreams

Goingbrokeaphobia – fear of losing all your money and needing to live with your mother

Baddaughterphobia – fear that you'll be labeled "the bad seed"

Name the Phobia	Describe It
Auntbigmouthphobia	The fear of hearing my aunt tell everyone, "I told you she would fail."

Name the Phobia	Describe It

COURAGE

EXERCISE #2

What am I afraid of? How can I respond in a way that builds my courage?

Your Fears and Phobias*	Your Courageous Response
People will laugh at me.	Maybe at first, but most will be supportive.
I will fail.	I am smart and have been successful more often than I've failed.

Your Fears and Phobias*	Your Courageous Response

COURAGE

EXERCISE #3

List messages that would help you be or act courageous and who could provide that message.

Message	From
"You can do it."	Father
"You have overcome other obstacles."	Mentor/Sponsor
"You are more than a conqueror."	Friend

COURAGE IS KEY

THINGS TO REMEMBER

- Courage is the water that nourishes your seed of greatness.

- Without courage, the dream will remain a vague picture that comes to light only while you sleep.

- Shame and blame are toxic twins that thrive on your silence.

- Face the things that you fear. Every time we face our fears, stare them down, and outlast or outlive them, we grow exponentially stronger.

- "You don't need a wishbone, you need backbone." –Joyce Meyer[33]

- It is impossible to grow into whom God meant you to be when you wake up every day scared and anxious.

- Doing what's difficult, frightening, and risky is the key to courageous actions.

- Courage makes it possible to achieve the things that once seemed impossible.

PART II:

THE SIX KEYS

CHAPTER 3

THE FIRST KEY: THE WORTHY GOAL

We must be able to describe what success look like if we hope to achieve it. "I'll just drive around until I find a street that looks like the one I'm looking for" leads to walking a dark street asking winos for directions or hoping to find a gas station because you've run out of gas, literally and figuratively. The sad truth is, when the tank is empty, "here" may have to be good enough. It doesn't have to be. The destination gives us the direction.

> *"Your goals are the road maps that guide you and show you what is possible for your life."*[34]

> – Les Brown

WISH BIG OR STAY HOME

"Knowing what I want is more important than wanting what I know."

Passion, the desire to do or be something that brings you joy, and courage, the ability to weather internal and external storms, can carry you a long way, but at some point, you must find a goal worthy of your efforts. Imagine you are Emily, Jessica, or Sophia.

Emily Needs a Job

Emily sits at home, unemployed, with diminishing resources. The last time she studied for an exam was thirteen years ago, when she got her driver's license. Today her goal is to get a job. With pressure from creditors and family members, this is a reasonable, realistic, and appropriate ambition.

She puts on the shoes she bought when she was going to join the gym (she didn't) and walks to a fast-food place. She fills out one application there or a hundred applications at the "apply-today-start-tomorrow" businesses. She's hired! She's reached her goal, but something is missing.

If you are happily working in one of these places, that's wonderful. However, if you are willing to invest your time, sweat, and effort to reach your destination, I am not sure "Welcome to Hi-Town" is it. If a nametag and a paper hat isn't enough, ask, "What's missing?"

Jessica Finds Her Husband

"I am through with single life. I'm ready to get married."

If that is your goal, go to Las Vegas and drink several shots of tequila and two or three glasses of Jägermeister.® If you do this three weekends in a row, it is very likely that by the end of the third visit, you will wake up beside a man whose name you will find alongside yours on the marriage license prominently displayed on the dresser. When he awakens, introduce yourself, and prepare to live as wife and husband.

For my lesbian and gay friends, substitute Fire Island or Palm Springs for Las Vegas and replace Cesar's Palace with Dinah Shore or the White Party. There may or may not be a marriage license on the dresser, but you'll be wearing matching rings, which may or may not be on your fingers. No matter the sexual orientation, you will need to go through the same introduction. Is this the destination you had in mind?

Sophia Buys a House

Sophia is watching Saturday morning TV and notices an ad with blissful singles and couples singing the praises of home ownership. They say that, like Sophia, they never thought they would be able to own a home. Like them, she can buy a house that she can pass down to her children and grandchildren. All she has to do is follow Big Bill's "Home in a Minute" plan. It will help her buy a house for no money down, and the payments will be lower than the rent she currently pays.

Sophia's KISS (Keep It Simple, Sista) plan is to buy one of those homes. She makes calls and finds a group willing to sell her a home and allow her to pay the interest only. Through a special, first-time homebuyer program, she ends up with an extra $4000 in her pocket, and magically, she is a homeowner.

Fast forward a year, eighteen months, or two years—you choose the amount of time. You know what is going to happen to Emily, Jessica, and Sophia.

Emily's wages don't cover her debt. She's sick of being the oldest fry cook on the night shift. Her feet hurt, her uniform doesn't fit, and the paper hat has left a permanent mark on her forehead.

Jessica's husband doesn't look good in the light of day. He has a girlfriend back home who is threatening to pay her a visit and the only husband qualification he has is a Y chromosome. To make matters worse, her friends posted the wedding photos with the caption "Friends don't let friends wed – LOL."[35]

Sophia's late with the mortgage payment. The interest rates have risen on her loan, and she can no longer afford the payments. She borrowed against the property to pay off some credit card debt, and now she has two mortgages. Within two years of her purchase, she is in foreclosure and has even more credit card debt from her original cards, plus the new ones they sent her once she was a "homeowner."

If you are living the Emily, Jessica, or Sophia story, is this the avenue of your dreams or another dead-end street? Emily has a job, but not a career or a future. Jessica has a spouse, but feels no closer to the love for which she hoped, and Sophia now lives in her sister's attic.

If you are disappointed when you realize that what you have is not what you wanted, you are not alone. The dead-end street is littered with thousands of your neighbors and friends: people who identified their goals as buying a house, finding a husband, or getting a job, and who now find themselves deep in debt, depression, or ill-fitting uniforms. They may feel like they've failed. They haven't. And neither have you.

A proverb says, "A stumble may prevent a fall."[36] This may be the perfect step at this juncture of your journey. It may be exactly the *stumble* needed to start your forward progress—to move you from static to active. If you recognize yourself in any of these stories, you are ready to plot a course that will move you closer to what is really stirring in your heart.

Although the first key isn't the most difficult of the six to achieve, it may be the hardest one to get right the first time. Why? You think you need a KISS (Keep it Simple, Sista), but what you need is SASSY.

BUILD A SASSY PLAN

"People are more likely to make progress on goals that are broken into concrete, measurable actions, with some kind of structured accountability and positive reinforcement."[37]

If you were preparing for a three-week vacation to a city with a very different climate you would develop a plan and make a list of items to take—bathing suits or hand warmers, boots or flip-flops. You'd probably watch the Weather Channel® to see what you might encounter and ask for advice from friends who have been to your destination. Today, you're embarking on a multiyear journey. The stakes are higher than any vacation you will ever take. You need a plan, and it should be SASSY: **S**ignificant, **A**chievable, **S**pecific, **S**atisfying, and **Y**ours.

SIGNIFICANT

This is the journey of your choosing. It's your life and your future, your dreams and your desires. Any goal that requires the kind of effort for which you're signing has to be significant ("having a major or important effect").[38] Fitting into size 10 jeans by next Tuesday may be important. However, it is not significant, or important enough to keep you from standing outside Krispy Kreme donuts waiting for the "Hot" sign rather than going to the gym or out for a walk.

Your goal has to be important enough to buy foods from the fruits and vegetable aisle and avoid the cookies, and your dedication has to last longer than your manicure. If for the next ten days, you drink only diet supplements on the pharmacy shelves, you can reach the size 10 goal, but about an hour after you take those jeans off, you'll be racing back to your size 14s, feeling ashamed and like a failure.

Like Jessica ("Wish Big or Stay Home"), your goal isn't your name on a marriage license. You want someone with whom you'll share your life, dreams, challenges, and future. You don't want to invest in something that fades as quickly as your spray tan. You want something worthy of your efforts, not a temporary fix. You're looking for someone who will love, honor, and cherish you after the vows, when you have the flu and don't look your best. We're talking about doing something that brings you joy today and for years to come.

THE "SIGNIGIANT" EXERCISE

To decide if the goal is significant, consider the following:

	Yes	No
Is it important enough for me to work on it when I'm tired, hungry, have PMS, or juggling family issues? When it's late at night or early in the morning?		
Will I work on it when I would rather go to out and play, sleep in, or watch the final sixteen episodes of *Law & Order* or a *Game of Thrones* marathon?		
Is it important enough for me to delay immediate gratification? To get me to walk past the alluring Sale and BOGO signs or pass up the butter croissants?		
Am I convinced that the results of my labor will be worth the efforts?		

If the answers are "Yes," the goal is probably significant enough to warrant the dedication and hard work. If not, dig a little deeper.

ACHIEVABLE

You've chosen a significant goal. Is it achievable? "Is it realistic and possible for me, given my skills, abilities, temperament, and strengths?" An achievable goal has to have an 80% or better chance of happening because of your efforts. Achievable does not mean easy; in fact, your effort should reflect the worthiness of the ambition and effort you will put forth to reach it. However, finding a goal that plays to your strengths, not one built on your weaknesses, will increase the likelihood of success. As Marcus Buckingham said in *Now Discover Your Strengths*, "You will excel only by maximizing your strengths, never by fixing your weaknesses."[39]

For example, I could set a goal of becoming a neurosurgeon. I'd need to go to medical school, finish an internship, and complete a residency at a top hospital. This meets the first requirement of a SASSY goal: it is significant. It is not, however, achievable. It is unrealistic and will likely end in failure because:

- I can't stay in school for longer than a semester at a time.

- I hate science, blood, cutting things, and sharp objects.

- I won't attend classes if the weather is nice.

- I'm not precise or meticulous and tend to drift off in the middle of things.

So even if everyone thinks I'd make a great neurosurgeon, and I set my sights on that as my destination, it's a bad idea whose time will never come. A great goal is one that is a match for what you need to do or learn and who you are.

THE "ACHIEVABLE" EXERCISE

	Yes	No
Can I master the majority of the requirements?		
Do I have the temperament to do or learn what is required?		
Will education, practice, and or coaching allow me to achieve this goal?		

You want to make sure you are suited to your goal. Is it enough to have a plan that is significant and achievable, or is there more? Yes, much more.

SPECIFIC

Now you are ready to focus on the details of your plan. Make sure your goal is clearly articulated and easy to measure. To be specific, you must:

- Define what you want to accomplish,
- Clearly outline how you will achieve it, and
- Have measurements and an established time frame.

Here are two examples of a specific goal.

As a part of her resolution to move from sedentary to active, Barbara decided to train for and complete a marathon, something no one in her circle of friends ever accomplished. She'd been a jogger for years, so she knew this was a serious challenge, mentally and physically. She selected the Nike Women's Marathon because at the end, she would receive a Tiffany® medal, and she loved great jewelry. Barbara gave herself a year and a half to go from running thirty minutes a day to running five hours, a time she could reasonably expect to achieve.

It was important that she did not say, "I'm going to run more," because that might be easy to achieve, but not worthy of much effort, and although this was a rung on the ladder of her greater goal of living a healthy life, it was not specific. Specificity required her to develop a mile-by-mile plan to complete the 14.19-meter run in about five hours. She established time and distance goals for each of the eighteen months leading up to the marathon. She put together a list of equipment she needed to buy (running shoes, anti-blister socks, and clothing), with purchase dates based on when she needed them. Her goal was significant, achievable, and specific.

Selena's goal was different. She is a gifted violinist. Playing, teaching, and listening to music made her feel alive. Her goal was to make a living and build a life around music. Like many of you, her first priority was to pay the rent. Fortunately, she had a job that did not break her spirit, but neither did it satisfy the longing in her heart.

Initially she thought her only choice was to quit her job and find something in the music field - she'd had very little success doing this in the past, or resign herself to working twenty years until she could retire, and then live her dream. She clearly had the gift, the passion, and the courage. She needed the plan. The more we talked, the clearer her plan became. She decided to work towards having 25% of her annual income come from her music over the next five years. Twenty-five percent translated into a dollar amount that seemed both possible and gratifying. She developed a chart showing the ways she could earn income—private lessons, weddings, and social events, and the pricing and timing needed for each event to reach her goal. She engaged friends to develop marketing materials and set up a website to help drive clients to her services.

Her path was clear. She knew what she needed to do and when it would happen. This gave her the confidence she needed to overcome the tough times and savor the good ones. You need to be able to see where you have been and where you are going. Your efforts have to result in something of value and importance and must be measurable.

THE "SPECIFIC" EXERCISE

Your goal is specific if you can establish a timeline that tells you what and when.

Timing	What	Other Information
Next 3-6 Months		
Next 6-12 Months		
Next 12-18 Months		
Next 18-24 Months		

You have made sure your resolution is significant, achievable, and specific. These three characteristics are focused on the goal. For those of us who have spent years being disappointed, it is imperative that it is also satisfying, which is not about the goal, but how you will feel when you accomplish it.

SATISFYING

In the SASSY plan, "satisfying" is personal. It is the "what's-in-it-for-me" factor: something rewarding beyond the pot of gold at the end of the rainbow. Ask yourself, "Why do I want to change from a diet filled with sugar and fats to one that includes antioxidants, vegetables, fruits, and low-fat meats? What will it say to me, about me, when my morning routine includes a visit to the gym or a brisk walk at lunchtime? How will I feel about myself when I look at the closing documents on my first home after bringing my credit score from pathetic to respectable?"

Perhaps your reward is the feeling of control you get as you pursue lifestyle changes. When I trained for my second marathon, the satisfaction wasn't in the miles I ran; they just hurt and seemed stupid. It was in the feeling that being disciplined gave me. I was rewarded by accomplishing something I didn't have to do, sometimes didn't want to do, and knew that many others could not make themselves do. If the aspiration is fulfilling, the journey will be, too. The small steps toward the goal pleased me. I had a daily calendar for my runs. When I completed a scheduled activity—a long run, cross training, or resting—I put an "X" through the day. That small act was gratifying, and although I knew it was not the end, it kept me going. Make sure your goal satisfies something in you, rewards you, and makes you smile at least some of the time.

You're not doing this for someone else—not for your children, your parents, neighbors, or friends. Make sure you have a great answer to "What's in it for me?"

THE "SATISFYING" EXERCISE

How does accomplishing this goal satisfy a wish or a longing (e.g., I've always wanted to do something no one in my family has done.)?

Describe the reward this goal provides.(e.g., I'll have bragging rights at the next family dinner).

The final leg of the SASSY plan is for those of you who have spent your lives taking care of others: children, parents, co-workers, friends, or pets.

YOURS

American preacher, televangelist, and author Joel Osteen said, "God has deposited a gift, a treasure inside you. Your destiny…excites you. Your destiny will be a part of what is in your heart—part of your very nature."[40] This means that the goal has to be about *you*, for *you*, and important to *you*. It can't be inherited from your mother, father, sister, great aunt, or anyone else.

Imagine your grandmother always wanted to operate a resale shop but couldn't because she had to have a steady income to support her family and pay the bills. She told you how proud she would be to have a little shop that the two of you could run together. You inherited the "we-should-open-a-resale-shop" goal, but you hate second-hand clothes, shoes, bags, and hats. No matter how hard you try, you are probably not going to be wildly successful in this endeavor because it is not your dream. It's like wearing your mother's shoes when you were four; no matter how beautiful they were, they just didn't fit.

This is crucial to your journey. No one wants to sacrifice, study, work evenings, and dedicate weeks and months to a goal that isn't tied to a gift that is *personal*. Make sure that whatever destination you choose is right for you and moves your spirit—that it is for and about you. Do not spend your energy trying to be great in someone else's life while letting your magnificent gifts fade away. This is your plan. It's SASSY: Significant, Achievable, Specific, Satisfying, and Yours.

GIVE IT TIME

"Focus on the journey, not the destination."[1]

To achieve something important and significant, you need to remind yourself that this journey takes real, measurable time. Give it time. Not the kind of time you think will miraculously appear between appointments, phone calls, and Twitter postings. Personal change worthy of this level of focus and effort takes years.

View this as a five- to seven-year journey because you don't want to add another thing that makes you feel bad, inadequate, or more stressed than you already are. Give yourself a break. Quiet the voices of "should." You should be working on your project, even though your mother is ill, your seventeen-year-old believes she's grown, and your dog has fleas. Remember that whatever you don't accomplish today can and maybe should be done tomorrow.

Knowing it will take time to achieve something significant allows you to gather resources, understand the size of the challenge, develop contingency plans, and prepare. I didn't know how connected planning and preparation were to the joy of reaching a goal until I ran my first marathon.

One ordinary day, I decided to run the Boston Peace Marathon. The marathon was my way of releasing anger and bolstering my ego; less than one percent of the population completes a marathon. I had six months to prepare to run 26.2 miles (42.19 kilometers), but because I had been a recreational runner since I was a teenager, I was confident I could do it. I found a program online that provided a road map: *Completing Your First Marathon in Only Six Months.* I was on my way. Six months after I began my training, I stood at the start line with hundreds of other runners.

At mile fifteen, pain and fatigue caused me to question the wisdom of my quest for marathon greatness. At mile eighteen, I did the math and thought I only had six miles to go—a sure sign my brain was oxygen-starved. At mile twenty, I prayed that a car would run over me so I could gracefully quit. Who could blame me for stopping to get into an ambulance? At mile twenty-three, I saw a person drop to the ground. Her legs folded like card table chairs. I envied her. I could not put any pressure on my quadriceps. For weeks after I finished the race, every cell in my body hurt!

I ran more than 500 miles training, and 26.2 on marathon day, and I did not enjoy more than thirty feet of it. I learned that shortcuts and big dreams seldom work well together. I also discovered that six months is not enough time for me to do something this tough and do it well. Yes, I finished, but in the end, there was no joy or satisfaction.

Doing something difficult and important takes more than six months. Sure, I finished the marathon and have the medal to prove it, but I never took the time to enjoy the journey, and it was agonizingly painful. As you choose your destination, remember it is an adventure into excellence. This is true of every goal worthy of your effort.

When I started writing this book, I thought I would finish it in a year—two at most. It's taken almost ten years. An important "ah-ha" for me was when I realized that there are months when I can do something every day, when I can focus hours of energy, making visible progress toward the destination, and there are months when I am lucky if I have time to write a page or read a single article. It was comforting to know that I had years to achieve my dream of completing this.

Allow yourself the time necessary to make changes, embrace movement toward what's important to you, and believe in the power of your passion, courage, and faith. I like to think of it as five years with an annual focus.

Year 1 – Finding the Seed and the Soil

Year 2 – Bringing the Water

Year 3 – Nurturing the Seedling

Year 4 – Grow, Prune, Bless

Year 5 – Reaping the Fruit

"No, no, no! I don't have years," you shout at the pages. "I need this (the house, the smaller waist, the love of my life) now!"

Where are you going to be in 1,826 days (five years)? Very likely, the answer is, "In the same chair I'm sitting in now." The great thing is that between now and the time you die, you've all the time in the world.

I hear a few of you saying, "It's too late. I'm too far in debt, too far gone. I've made too many mistakes. I'll never achieve health, do work I am passionate about, or find the love I desire, and I don't have five years to dedicate to changing." Maybe you believe that you don't have much time because you don't think you will be alive in five years. It is true that a small percentage of you who are reading this will not be alive five years from now. A very, very small percentage.

Are you willing to bet your future that you will be one of the dearly departed and continue speeding down the road to Less, a town just north of Apathy? Are you? Chances are you will lose that bet, and five years from now, you will be alive and no closer to your dream. I have cancer, and I'm betting I'll be here, so you might want to rethink your exit plan. The truth about time is that it will pass—quickly and slowly—ready or not. You have time to accomplish the goal you've worked so hard to identify and truthfully, you have time to enjoy the journey.

ENJOY THE JOURNEY

"You are the designer of your destiny. You are the author of your story."[42]

When doing research on what you will need in order to purchase your first home at a reasonable interest rate you learn that you have to develop an attractive credit picture. Don't start every internal conversation with, "I hate that I have to live like this." Look for interesting opportunities to do things that will support your journey, and don't focus on the endless list of what you are missing. The mind remembers bad things more easily than good things. Focus on the good things like the neighbor who agreed to help you understand credit bureau ratings.

If it takes five years to build inheritable wealth through real estate, those 1,826 days can be either (a) an interesting, fun, exciting, and challenging trek filled with memories you want to share or (b) scars on your psyche and memories that haunt your nightly dreams. Choose "a."

Enjoy the journey.

It's the journey of your choosing. Think of it as a vacation with good days, great days, and a few hours you may want to forget, instead of the life of Sisyphus,[43] pushing a large rock up the hill every morning, only to watch it roll down in the evening, knowing that you must push it up again, for all eternity.

Enjoy the trip because this is your life. You are the artist, the singer, the homeowner, or the entrepreneur. It's not a task or a trial; it's you doing something you want to do, traveling to a place you have long wanted to visit, or realizing a dream painted on your soul.

Enjoy the journey

If it is your decision to go from waking up on the couch with potato chip crumbs on your sleep shirt to living a habitually healthy lifestyle, don't start every day with dread, convincing yourself that the only way to health is to crawl through the community garden eating wheat grass and beets. Reaching your goal is not going to be a short jaunt to the supermarket; it's a long and sometime arduous adventure that will have joyful times you would never have imagined. And as with any worthy goal, it is an adventure of years, not weeks.

THE "GOAL" EXERCISE

Find a quiet place. Allow your heart to guide you to your answers. Don't censure yourself. There are no "right" or "wrong" answers.

1) What is my destination, resolution, or goal?

If you hear yourself saying, "I can't think of anything," keep asking the same questions until you feel free enough to move forward. The goal might change as you become clearer about your passion. This is an exercise to help you learn to pay attention to your feelings and listen to your voice.

2) Is it SASSY?

	Yes	No
Is it significant?		
What makes it significant?		
Is it achievable?		
Which/what skills and abilities make it achievable?		
Is it specific?		
List three ways it is specific.		
Is it satisfying?		
What need, desire, or resolution does it satisfy?		
Is it yours?		
What makes it yours?		

Remember: This, like you and I, is a work in progress. Continue sitting with the questions. Perfection is unlikely and a waste of time, or an excuse go to Dairy Queen.®

THE FIRST KEY

THINGS TO REMEMBER

- Don't wish "small."

- Focus on the "what" before jumping to the "how" and "when."

- There is no "get rich quick" scheme in your future.

- Build a SASSY plan—(Significant, Achievable, Specific, Satisfying, and Yours).

- Look for interesting opportunities to do things that will support your journey.

- Never settle for another's definition of what you should have, do, or be.

- Your past is not your future. Your past is finished, over, and can never be undone or changed.

- Any worthy goal is an adventure of years, not weeks.

CHAPTER 4

THE SECOND KEY: BEHAVE LIKE YOU MEAN IT

How you act and what you do defines what is important. If you say health is important, you have to put the sugar cookies, pork rinds, and soda back on the grocery shelves. Although some would say you could eat them in moderation, you know they're not talking to or about you. How you behave is the action that leads you to achieve the things that are important to you.

"The best day of your life is the one on which you decide your life is your own. The gift is yours - it is an amazing journey - and you alone are responsible for the quality of it. This is the day your life really begins."[4]

- Bob Mowad

ALIGN YOUR WISHES & WILLS

"You can't talk yourself out of problems you behave yourself into."[45]

You've identified the seed given to you by the Divinity; the soil, your passion, gathered your courage; the water that will nourish you passion and found a goal worthy of your efforts. The Second Key is matching your behaviors to your desires and wishes. A young mother tells me she hopes her three-year-old daughter will sleep on the flight we are waiting to board. She takes a bag of candy from her purse and hands it to the little girl. The mom's behavior does not match her desires. What about you?

Whatever you uncover and discover to be worthy of pursuing has to match what you're willing to do to have it. Here's why.

You're walking along the beach with your daughter. You see a magnificent home with stairs carved from the rocks that lead from the patio to the ocean. There's a huge picture window reflecting an incredible sunset. You meet the owner, who tells you that she always wanted have a place on the ocean—one she could pass on to her children and grandchildren.

You call your sister and describe the house and the view.

"Sis, I wish I had that house. It has this incredible view, a wrap-around porch in the front, and it's in a quiet neighborhood with great schools."

But is "I wish..." really true?

A week later, you buy those $320 boots at the over-priced store next to your office because there's no point trying to save for that house. You tell yourself that it's so far from possible that it's ridiculous to even start down that road. Your wishes and your will don't match. There is no backbone with your wishbone.

What you spend time doing indicates what you value. Do you spend hours looking at the Fall Collection of Via Spiga® shoes and bags or your credit report? Your efforts and energy determine your destination. You say you want one thing, but what will you do to go from the run-down apartment in the deteriorating neighborhood to the home of your dreams? Aligning wishes and wills can seem like a daunting task, but it's crucial for long-term success.

DO WHAT MATTERS

"If you want a new life you have to have a new lifestyle."[46]

The Second Key may be the most difficult, because success is rooted in the actions that demonstrate what you will to do in order to achieve your wishes. It's the walking of your talk.

Indifference or a lack of commitment to achieve your stated goal makes the probability of success extremely low. I won't say it's zero because we know people who have succeeded in spite of their efforts, but truthfully, it's not likely to be you or me. What kind of effort will it require? The simple answer: when your children are with their grandmother, you may be completing an online course or attending a mixer to build your network. This is the action behind your passion.

Doing what matters means that if you say you want to live a healthier lifestyle and are serious about becoming more active, you must get off the couch and walk the dog, go to the gym, or put the yoga DVD in and do the work. At least four days a week, you may have to get up an hour earlier to fix a healthy breakfast and prepare your lunch, and you may want to take a twenty-minute walk at lunchtime.

Stop looking for the magic product to reduce your waistline while you sleep. No pill, pamphlet, or machine will do what thirty minutes on the treadmill or twenty minutes in the pool will do. Dr. Maya Angelou said, "Nothing will work unless you do."[47] You have to do the work.

When your friends are playing games on the Internet, you will be searching LinkedIn® for resources and contacts. While others are reading the Lifestyle or the Sports section, you're reading the Business section or researching new products. Commitment may mean less sleep as you design your website after the kids are in bed. It may mean entertaining a potential client after twelve hours at your day job.

To build inheritable wealth through real estate, you may have to spend Saturdays and Sundays combing through hundreds of online sites, driving to remote locations, or reading real estate exam study materials.

You may have to sing at the neighborhood bar's open mic nights after a late meeting in the office, likely wearing the same pantsuit and a pair of uncomfortable but sexy shoes you keep in the car.

To those who are watching and those who are partners in your journey, what you do and how you behave means much more than what you say. Your demonstrated commitment to change has to be evident in your daily behaviors throughout the journey. If you say you want to run a successful consulting firm or have a healthy lifestyle, you have to live in a way that others can follow.

If I ask your father, spouse, or best friend, "Why is Maria working so hard?" What would they say? Would they have no idea, or would they say that you are focused on getting into medical school to become a surgeon? Can everyone tell by your actions that you're determined to build your financial portfolio through real estate? If not, what story do your behaviors tell? The evidence always answers the question.

Long-lasting change requires diligence and a commitment to looking at everything you do through the lens of your goal—especially those things you value. This key is built on effort. Luckily, this is the work of your choosing. You need to have both a long- *and* a short-term outlook, to be able to view the horizon and watch for the cracks in the sidewalk. Often, when we make a resolution, we focus all of our energies on the future: the next milestone, the next call, the next five pounds, the next quarter, the next new product, proposal, or contract. On the journey, we miss the scenery, looking only at the road ahead. Today becomes unimportant, but today is all we have.

STAY IN THE NOW

"Yesterday is history. Tomorrow is mystery. Today is a gift, that's why it's called the present."[8]

Do you ever wake up feeling as if you are late before your feet touch the floor? Your day isn't two hours old, and you're already behind schedule. The problem is you're living in the future. One morning, it dawned on me that living in the future caused me to turn my back on the blessings God offered throughout the day—the joy on the face of the child playing with her aunt in the park, the happy, tail-wagging dog on his morning walk, and the magnificent pink clouds at sunset. Every day, there are things that make you laugh or smile—watching a child eating ice cream and remembering your little one's first time. There are moments that touch your heart—seeing a father combing his daughter's hair and knowing that Mom usually does it, but he's giving it everything because he wants her to look great and he loves his little girl.

Living in the future caused me to miss so much. Yes, the cancer made the Now much more important, but don't wait for something like that to get motivated. Starting today, take time to appreciate the Now. When I walk my dog, I let him wander and sniff. I love watching his excitement when we pass a squirrel or a cat. We're not on a mission; it's time to see him enjoy his life. Even when it's raining, I'm reminded that I don't melt, so I put on a slicker and we step in the puddles. Sure, it means drying us both off when we get home, but he loves the feel of the towel rubbing his fur, and even that chore makes me laugh.

I watch the sun rise over the mountains in Arizona and the ocean in Long Beach. I've trained myself to enjoy the moment. Sometimes it's difficult to do this. My cell phone starts to ring, and hordes of emails call my name. Maybe there are the lunches you need to fix, homework to check, or clothes to drop off at the cleaners. It's hard to stay present and do all the things it takes to reach your goal, but it's crucial to your mental, physical, and emotional health to pay attention to the small and important moments. Starting today, you must train yourself to do that.

When you send emails, ask how the reader is doing, or inquire about the vacation they had last month. Ask about their progress in getting their daughter into college. Read their reply as if it's a note from a friend.

Current research shows that human beings immediately judge others on two characteristics—warmth and competence.[49] If a person is warm, trustworthy, honest, and likable, we are more likely to listen to see if she is competent, smart, and capable of delivering on her promise. I wonder how many wonderful people you have missed connecting with because you didn't take the time to establish trust—people who could and would have helped you reach your destination.

Niki is one of those people in my life. I met Niki at a meeting with her staff members. She came in to introduce me to the team and then planned to leave. As we were getting to know one another, she mentioned that she'd been up early for a run. The conversation quickly turned to our mutual love of marathons. She was training for her first, and I told her to have someone at the finish line with a shot of tequila. It quickly dulls the pain and lifts the spirit. She said it was the best advice she's ever received.

We had full lives and schedules and shared a common insanity—running 26.2 miles.

Early in the pursuit to build a successful consulting firm, I would not have talked about marathons, except as a gateway to a sale. I would have convinced myself that she was a busy executive with little time for chitchat and moved quickly to secure the contract. I would have missed the significance of the Now, of hearing her excitement and fears about her first marathon.

We've become friends, colleagues, and support for one another. Her organization is one of my favorite clients. It's not the minutes before or those that follow that are important; it's *this* minute. It is not a dress rehearsal; it's your life.

THE "BEHAVIORS" EXERCISE

Find a quiet place. Be open, authentic, and honest as you answer the following questions.

What would my father, husband, or best friend say if someone asked, "Why is [Insert your name] working so hard? What is [Insert your name] working on?"

How would my friends, colleagues, and family members describe my goal(s)?

How am I using my strengths and gifts?

What weaknesses do I need to acknowledge so I can move forward?

THE SECOND KEY

THINGS TO REMEMBER

- Actions speak louder than words.

- Align your desired outcomes with your attitude and behaviors.

- Do the things that will have the greatest return on your investment.

- Don't focus on the future and ignore the present.

- Your efforts and energy determine your destination.

- Long-lasting change requires diligence and a commitment to looking at everything you do through the lens of your goal.

- What you spend time doing indicates what you value.

CHAPTER 5

THE THIRD KEY: GATHER GUIDES AND SUPPORTERS

Everyone needs help. Those who see themselves as strong and those who see themselves as weak share the same truth. "You can't do it alone." On the trip from homeless to successful homeowner, you will encounter obstacles that no single person can overcome. Somewhere along the way, you will need friends, family, strangers, and even competitors to provide guidance and support.

It takes a village to raise a child.

– African Proverb

SEEK GUIDANCE

No one who achieves success does so without ... the help of others.[50]

It may be difficult to accept that success cannot be achieved alone. No matter how focused and committed you are, you need individuals to help you stay on track, keep you motivated, and pick you up and dust you off when you stumble. Find people you can rely on to provide guidance, advice, and support at four p.m. or four a.m.

Possibly, not in the beginning, but between setting the goal and achieving excellence, you need a diverse group of supporters and guides. Guides point you in the direction of your goal. For guides to be beneficial, you must know where you're going and be able to articulate it in a way that allows them to be engaged and of service. They help you see when you're off course and then help you find your way back. They may be family members who send you to the Internet with a link that shows you how to increase funding for your start-up. Maybe they point you in a direction that opens doors to new resources, fuels your creativity, or shines a light on a missed path.

When do you seek guidance? When you wonder if what you are doing is taking you toward your goal or away from it. Seek guides when you're not sure whether you missed an important turn or piece of information. Seek guidance when you make a major decision. Look for those who have walked similar paths and are willing to share the secrets to navigating by the stars.

You and three friends decide to develop a global import business. On this journey, you start out on a paved highway—familiar, solid, clean, and relatively new. Then you turn onto a dirt road. The dust makes finding the markers difficult. You leave this road and enter a jungle—dark, complicated, with unfamiliar markers, and little to go on except your beliefs and values. It's not wise to venture into the wilderness alone. When this happens, you want people who can provide information to make the journey smoother. Find people who can help you understand the logistics and legal challenges.

When I was on safari in Kenya, we went looking for lions. There was a driver and a guide. The guide was native to the area. He knew how to read signs that none of us would ever notice along a road that none of us could see.

On the journey, when you're trying to figure out how to navigate unfamiliar and treacherous territory, find people who have gone into the woods and survived. Allow them to offer their insights. Don't dismiss them because they're not you, don't have your experiences, or have not achieved what you have. Guidance can come from many sources. Don't forget, along with a list of potential guides, you also need supporters.

GATHER SUPPORTERS

"When we give cheerfully and accept gratefully, everyone is blessed."[51]

Supporters are those you seek when you're at your wits' end. You may not know where that is today but when you find yourself there, call someone. Support may come from family members, colleagues, or the counter lady at the dry cleaners. Supporters are the friends you call to talk you out of eating the box of Girl Scout Thin Mints® hidden in the freezer under the broccoli. Supporters not only tell you to move away from the cookies, they offer to meet you in the driveway and go for a walk or bring you a Weight Watchers® brownie. They offer to meet you at the gym and call you when you don't feel like getting out of bed.

Your children can be an invaluable source of assistance, whether it is playing chase in the park with your five-year-old, basketball with your twelve-year-old, or Wii® Dance with your teen. All are inexpensive ways to spend time doing things that will benefit your mind, body, and spirit. Don't forget the people you see daily. The server at the donut shop can play an important role in helping you stay the course. He can serve you a bowl of fruit and a donut hole and offer encouragement. Your colleagues can support your goals through the restaurants they choose for lunch, the snacks they bring to meetings, and the treats they have on their desks.

Recently, Diana Nyad made history when, at age sixty-four, she completed the fifty-three-mile swim from Cuba to Florida.[52] This is a great story about setting and reaching a goal. It did not matter that she was sixty-four, it had never been done, or that she failed *four* times before. She set a goal and did the work she needed to do in order to be successful. As importantly, a thirty-five-person support team accompanied Ms. Nyad. I am sure there were times when she wanted to quit and someone on the support team provided encouragement at the precise moment she needed it.

Even if your goal is not as grand as Diana Nyad's—you've decided to replace your cookie addiction, weight gain, and bad cholesterol levels with a healthy lifestyle—you will need support. The more people with whom you share your goals, the greater the pressure is to stay on track. Your support team bolsters your confidence and rejuvenates your spirit.

FIND YOUR SHEILA

"To focus on your weaknesses isn't a sign of diligent humility. It is almost irresponsible. By contrast…the most honorable thing to do is face up to the strength potential inherent in your talents and then find ways to realize it."[53]

You've identified your strengths and chosen an achievable goal, given the skills and knowledge you have or can acquire. It is necessary to know what you do well and what you don't. Working from your strengths does not mean ignoring your weaknesses, especially when they interfere with your ability to keep your resolution. It means doing what you *can* and finding resources to do what you *cannot.*

When I established my consulting firm, I realized that I was accounting challenged. I didn't understand how to make or read a spreadsheet or reconcile numbers. I was great at selling and delivering the work but baffled by what it took to prepare tax receipts, process client invoices, or complete any of the accounting and organizing tasks needed to run the business. No amount of training, courses, coaching, or auditing would change my attitude or aptitude for sequential numbering. Even if I spent years working on my weaknesses, I would be at best well below average. The same amount of energy focused on my strengths would yield better results in less time with a lot less effort. The value of diversity is that I knew there was someone out there who loved doing what I could not, someone whose strengths partnered well with my weakness.

It was Sheila, a woman who loved organizing. Her strength and passion was helping those of us who number our invoices according to some cosmic feeling—"this invoice feels like #44837"—to find a better way. When she told me I should assign a number to a client and use a sequential system to track the client, the date, and the type of services, I was as amazed. as I imagine primitive people were every time they made fire.

When the day comes and you need to find your Sheila, run; don't walk. Perhaps you need to reduce the fats in your diet, but you are cooking challenged. When you read a cookbook, watch *Rachel Ray*,[54] or peruse the vegetable aisles at your supermarket, you come up with the same menu—chips and salsa. Your "Sheila" may be your cousin, who loves to cook and will make you healthy food for lunch and dinner.

It may be your neighbor, who is a stay-at-home dad. He makes healthy gourmet food for his family and is looking to make extra money doing what he loves. You can't afford to pay him? Offer to trade writing, carpentry, or math tutoring for food or find several friends he can work for and trade referrals for scrumptious vegetarian dishes.

Discover your strengths and natural gifts. Have faith that others can and will support you on your journey. Find those whose gifts match your gaps. They're ready to help.

ACCEPT HELP

*"It is not so much our friends' help that helps us,
as the confidence of their help."*[55]

People can only provide support if you are willing to accept their help. This may be difficult for you, especially if you were raised to view accepting help as a sign of weakness or character defect. Picture your role model, your mother, carrying six bags filled with toiletries, groceries, and dog treats—arms drooping and the veins in her neck showing the strain. Your neighbor asks if she needs a hand, and she replies, "No, I've got it."

When she sets the bags on the table, she can barely unfold her fingers to rub the deep red lines where the weight of the bags cut into her flesh. She looks at you and proudly says, "Women are strong and do not need help." This message can make it difficult for you to ask for help or accept it when it's offered.

Fast-forward twenty years; you're no longer the twelve-year-old watching her mother struggle with the groceries. You have put together a great team. Sharon, a wonderful woman you met at a recent business leaders' conference, says she's noticed you struggling with your marketing and asks if she can help. She did some marketing for her brother and enjoyed it. You want to accept her help, but the offer of help makes you extremely uncomfortable.

You hear your father's voice. "No one offers something for nothing. You don't know what she wants from you, and you don't want to be obligated to anyone."

You reply, "Thanks, but no, thank you. I'll figure it out." That's true, but at what price?

Along my journey, I had to accept offers of help. From the simple, "Can I help set up the room?" to the offer to introduce me to a CEO who became one of my largest clients. Is there a tit-for-tat, a give and get? Yes, but it has never been at the expense of my ethics or something that caused me to regret taking the help. Your mom may have taught you that you can't trust the extended hand, but you can unlearn that lesson.

How do you get help?

1. Accept help when it is offered.
2. Whenever possible, ask for suggestions and listen for answers and solutions to make your journey easier.
3. Solicit ideas in open settings and one-on-one meetings. View groups and individuals as knowledge and insight experts. Ask for and accept their input. Recognize that reaching your destination requires you to behave in ways that encourage people to support and guide you.
4. Develop a list of potential supporters and guides. Plan to add at least two names per month to both columns.

What's next? Grow your knowledge base as you expand your network. When you know where you are headed and you have the support and guidance to keep you on track, it's time to focus your energy on learning.

THE "GUIDES AND SUPPORT" EXERCISE

Make a list of people who can offer support and guidance.

Supporters	Guides
My sister Sharon	**The local realtor**

THE THIRD KEY

THINGS TO REMEMBER

- Reaching your destination requires allowing people to encourage and support you.

- Find those whose gifts match your gaps.

- Listen for experiences that will point out the best route.

- View groups and individuals as knowledge and insight experts.

- Supporters bolster your confidence and rejuvenate your spirit.

- Guides point you in the direction of your goal.

- Ask for suggestions and listen for experiences.

CHAPTER 6

THE FOURTH KEY: LEARN EVERYTHING

It is important to learn everything you can and to never stop learning. Management consultant and educator Peter Druker said, "Learning is a lifelong process of keeping abreast of change."[56] Along the way, you'll need information that you don't have—information that existed in the past or is just forming in the prefrontal cortex of a woman on the Isle of Mauritius.

"Before you become too entranced with gorgeous gadgets and mesmerizing video displays, let me remind you that information is not knowledge, knowledge is not wisdom, and wisdom is not foresight. Each grows out of the other, and we need them all."[57]

– Arthur Clarke

GET AN EDUCATION

"Learning is a treasure that will follow its owner everywhere."[58]

The fourth key focuses on the importance of learning and education. At many points along the way, you will need to do something new or something that requires expanded skills. You can accomplish this in many ways. You may find yourself in the classroom or working online, in the formal setting of the university or sitting around the table with your neighbors. With limited time and resources, whatever you do has to give you the skills that will make you successful.

When you don't know how to do something, it is easy to find a training program that will help you. In some cases, that may be what you need. When the answers can be acquired by repetition, training is a great option. However, I found that the power of training is limited. According to the Merriam-Webster Dictionary,[59] to train is to "form by instruction, discipline, or drill."[60] For the changes we're talking about, you may need an education, not simply training.

Here's how I learned the difference between training and education. I wanted to learn French. I was scheduled to make my first trip to Paris, and I'd heard they appreciated visitors who made an effort to speak the language. I bought a cassette series (yes, it was that long ago), and for several weeks as I drove to work, a gentleman on the tapes and I conversed. He would speak, and I would respond. Repetition worked. It was perfect. I could tell him that I was hungry and wanted to eat now. We greeted each other and introduced Mr. Green to Miss Smith. I could get a pencil and ask someone to close the door.

Somewhere on the plane between Boston and Paris, I lost my French. When I arrived in Paris, no one spoke the French that Mr. Tape and I spoke. The training I received was very different from the education I needed. Achieving excellence requires building and developing your talents, knowledge, and skills while living inside a kaleidoscope with a constantly changing landscape. Training can prepare you to begin the journey, but by itself, it will have limited success. The tapes can teach me to say "bonjour," but they do not prepare me to understand what the baggage claim manager at the airport is saying about my lost luggage.

On the journey from the body you hate to the healthy lifestyle of your dreams, one of your biggest challenges will be what you don't know. For example, you want to develop a healthy lifestyle, but the only thing you know is that a large of number of calories equals weight gain. You decide you need to burn more calories so you can still eat the high-calorie foods you crave. You notice that all the runners you see on TV are thin, and you choose running as your new calorie-burning exercise.

Your program consists of putting on a pair of athletic shoes you bought because they matched that incredibly cute top you purchased on your vacation in the Bahamas. You take off running down the hill in front of your house. The street ends next to the juice bar, where you pick up a "healthy" fruit smoothie (325 calories, 45g of sugar) and drink it as you walk back to your house. There's no way you can run up that hill and not spill your $6.30 drink.

But what you don't know can hurt you. The next morning, you are barely able to walk. The fronts of your legs ache. You have shin splints from running downhill on hard surfaces in the wrong shoes before you strengthened the muscles in your legs. This condition causes two things: first, the fronts of your legs ache for hours, and second, you abandon your exercise routine.

The Fourth Key is to know as much as possible about every aspect of your journey and plan. It's crucial to find out how much you don't know and then build your knowledge base. Where do you start?

Read articles on calories and foods. Talk with your sister-in-law about how she lost and maintained her weight for more than four years. Even if you think she's an idiot, she must be doing something that you can use.

If you think all runners are thin, go to the starting line at your local 5K (3.1 miles). If there are one hundred runners, eighty-five of them are not thin. Some are extremely not thin. Elite marathoners and Olympic distance runners are thin, but so are runway models, and most of them don't run.

If you decide you want running to be a part of your healthy routine, spend your first two months learning about the sport, the equipment, and your body. Learn the difference between pronating and supination. Join a running club. Find supporters and guides (see Chapter 5 - The Third Key: *Gather Guides & Supporters*).

A healthy lifestyle is more than any single action. Build in enjoyable family events. Take a trip to the beach and go for a jog with the dog or run with your ten-year-old as she roller blades on the bike path. Ask your seventeen-year-old to plot two, four, and six-mile paths from computer-generated GPS programs. Have your mother or sister-in-law fix you pre-and-post run snacks.

On family nights, play Scrabble using only food and exercise words. Schedule family outings that include hiking, swimming in the lake, and bike trips. In the winter, ice-skating, cross-country skiing, and pulling the sled with your little one on it are great exercises. These experiences are fun and can easily be modified to delight even the pickiest family member.

Maybe you are passionate about creating inheritable wealth for future generations. You've seen infomercials advertising how easily people who started with nothing ("OMG, they're talking to me!") made six thousand dollars in the first month and were on their way to becoming millionaires. You send for the DVD, CDs, books, tests, and testimonials. The twelve-pound box arrives. You open it and discover you don't even know how to load the information onto your computer. Your middle-school child loads it, and voila, you're watching a handsome man with a deep, sexy voice talking about ARMs, due-on-sale clauses, escrow disbursements, guaranty, revolving liability, and sweat equity (which is the one thing that sounds familiar). You have a DVD you don't understand, CDs that have you more confused after listening than you were before, and a "pre-test" that only serves to frighten you to death.

You put the software disks and booklets back in the box, set it on the floor about three feet from another box filled with things you don't understand, place a piece of plywood over them, cover it with a table cloth you found during spring cleaning, and you have a table.

The problem? What you don't know is exponentially greater than what you do know. You are not sure where to get the answers to the questions you can't form. It isn't your will; it's your skill. That's why the Fourth Key is so important. Continuous learning translates into behaviors and actions that build your skill base, one knowledge brick at a time. It means starting where you are, not where your skinny, running-obsessed neighbor and the smooth-talking Infoguy are.

Want to learn about real estate? Start with the basics. There are great government pamphlets written in easy-to-understand terms. If you find a term that you don't understand, go online to the millions of sites that can define it in hundreds of ways, one of which will work for you. Find a friend, relative, neighbor, hairdresser, or dog walker who's studying the housing market and barter for knowledge. If you make great cookies, offer to bake for their kids' birthday in exchange for their help finding you the best cities for home purchases. Perhaps you or your spouse can exchange simple auto repair for a quick course in financing dos and don'ts. Keep a record of what you learn because two years from now when you need it, it is not wise to depend on your aging brain. At least, that's my experience.

MATCH STYLES & INFORMATION

"Live as if you were to die tomorrow. Learn as if you were to live forever."[61]

Continuous learning and education can take many forms: community college, the Internet, audio and video resources, books, magazines, local lecture series, brown-bag lunches, seminars, networking events, and external conferences. These are just a few of the ways everyone can learn and develop new skills and knowledge. Remember, individuals learn differently; some are visual, others auditory or experiential.

The visual learners in the family will enjoy learning from the Internet, books, and DVDs. You can drop them off at Barnes & Nobles, and they'll thank you. Audio learners may want to attend seminars and speaker series or to listen to information they download to their smart phone or tablet. The experiential learners in the family can be sent out with a pedometer to find the route that will burn the calories in a Snickers bar. You know you're going to eat at least one between now and 2020!

Everyone involved in the destination has to be involved in the education. If you've decided to eat healthy foods that increase the quality and quantity of your life, it is important that everyone in the household become knowledgeable food shoppers. Younger members can create food charts. Your teenagers can have a scavenger hunt in the grocery store to find the healthiest snack foods on sale. Your friends can share recipes for delicious, healthy dishes. Your colleagues can encourage you by calculating the calories burned walking from the furthest spot in the parking lot.

Education is more than instruction, discipline, or drill. It has breadth and depth. It provides information that shapes what we know and how we behave. It provides us with skills and will—experiences and information. Education is key to success because it fills the head with information, teaches the hands to act, and opens the heart to believe in the joy of the journey.

THE "LEARN EVERYTHING" EXERCISE

Find a quiet place. Don't let shame or disappointment about what you don't know interfere with your plans to succeed. The important thing is to identify what you need to know and your plan to learn it.

What do I need to learn today, in the next six months, and in the next year?

What are some uncommon learning opportunities (e.g., working at a booth at the local swap meet to learn how to price products or helping a realtor with an open house in trade for an hour of coaching on negotiating with realtors)?

Where can I find learning material unique to my destination?

THE FOURTH KEY

THINGS TO REMEMBER

- Have a learning and an education mindset.

- Your biggest challenges will be what you don't know. Find out how much you don't know and then build your knowledge base.

- Education can be formal or informal, academic or experiential, self-paced, virtual, or facilitator led.

- Learn as much as possible about every aspect of your journey.

- Education has breadth and depth. It provides information that shapes what we know and how we behave.

- Everyone involved in the destination has to be involved in the education.

- Build your skill base one knowledge brick at a time.

CHAPTER 7

THE FIFTH KEY: ARE WE THERE YET?

We measure what is important and valuable. We track our children's growth on the wall. We get on the scales at the mall, the gym, and in our mother's bathroom. We calculate how far, how long, how many, and how much. Measurements and deliverables tell us how well we are doing and how close we are to achieving our goal.

"What gets measured gets done."[62]

– Tom Peters

WHY I SPEED

"Setting goals is the first step in turning the invisible into the visible."[63]

The Fifth Key is establishing measurements and deliverables. Spending time determining what you want to measure and why, is worth the effort. If you know why you are doing something, it is easier to figure out how to quantify progress.

I know why I speed. When I travel on interstate roads in California, I observe the speed limit. I do this because when I didn't, each of the three speeding tickets I received came with an increasingly negative financial burden. It is different on the drive from California to Las Vegas Nevada.

When I cross the state line and enter Nevada, I feel like I am free to drive as fast as I want. I don't remember posted speed signs, and even if there were signs, I've never seen anyone get a ticket. My guess, if you got a speeding ticket on your way to gamble, it would cause you to turn around and go home. After all, how lucky can you be if you get a $500 fine before you arrive at the roulette table?

I drive much faster in Nevada than I do in California, even though I know that the danger of having an accident is much higher when driving fast. My safety does not determine my speed, the only thing that matters is what gets measured.

Whatever your goal, it is essential that there are clear success measurements and deliverables. We live in a goal-centered world. We set the goal of losing weight for the college reunion and measure progress daily. Parents know the time it takes to get from the office to the daycare center. We calculate miles per gallon, calories burned during sex, and productivity per employee. We are a culture of metrics. It's a universal obsession. Because this is true, you must decide what you want to measure, why, and how. Measurements, because they tell us what we value, are important elements in achieving excellence.

Next up – determining the *right* things to measure. If you are not mindful, you may end up measuring what is easy, not important. This can lead to a false sense of completion or failure.

MY CHOLESTEROL IS 460?

"Good questions outrank easy answers."[64]

Imagine that I go to the doctor to have my annual physical. My cholesterol level comes back a whopping 375. I go to my ninety-year-old father,[65] who has seen family members die from the results of high cholesterol, and tell him that I'm worried about my health. He says he saw a TV program that showed that exercise could significantly lower cholesterol levels. He offers to pay me five dollars every time I go to the gym—a small but significant amount for my father.

Week #1, I get fifteen dollars for my visits to the gym on Monday, Wednesday, and Friday. The next week, and for ten weeks after that, I receive twenty dollars for four visits per week. Three months after the first cholesterol screening, my father accompanies me to the doctor's office. My blood is drawn, and through the miracle of medical science, the results arrive in minutes. My new and updated cholesterol has gone from an unhealthy 375 to 460. (Don't send me with accurate medical information, you get the point!) My father is livid. He accuses me of lying about my gym visits and demands a refund.

I didn't lie. Every day that I said I went to the gym, I did. I measured gym visits. However, there is a Starbucks® on the corner next to my gym. On my way to the gym, I buy a vente mocha frappuccino (whole milk, please) with extra whip cream. Then I cross the street to the local Krispy

Kreme.® donut shop. Ordering one donut is silly, so I order two. The kid behind the counter asks if I want three (at a 10% discount), and when I say sure, he tells me that for only a few pennies more, I can buy a half dozen. So being my father's financially responsible daughter, I buy six hot donuts. I take the warm donuts and my icy frappuccino into the sauna at the gym. The warmth of the steam keeps the donuts moist, and the icy frappuccino keeps me cool. Going to the gym yields a cholesterol level of 460. As Lillian says to Annie in *Bridesmaids*, "You're your problem, and you're your solution."[66]

Even if you're not cheating, getting the goal right is important for you and everyone who tries to support you. Here's why. Elena eats cookies by the bagful. At least once a year, when she realizes she can no longer fit into her sweat pants, she decides to lose weight. To do this, she resolves to give up cookies, which, she professes, are the reason she is gaining weight.

Within a week, the only thing she can think about is cookies. She becomes irritable, unhappy, and angry, feelings she blames on the lack of cookies. Over the next several weeks, she becomes depressed because she doesn't lose weight and she realizes that removing cookies from her diet is not leading to success. There are two reasons this is true.

First, she removes only cookies from her diet. She continues to consume all of her usual comfort foods: French-fries, ice cream, and bagels with butter and strawberry jam. And, she eats them at the same times of day, just before bedtime. She also increases the amount of wine she drinks. After all, she has to do something to help her sleep now that she doesn't have her nightly cookie coma.

Second, everyone around her gives her cookie substitutes - candy, chips, and anything else they can find because she's a pain, and it's easier than listening to her whine. Besides, this is an annual event, and they know she'll eventually go back to cookies—and the sooner the better. Does this sound familiar?

What is a better metric to move you toward your goal of getting healthier and slimmer? You can buy a pedometer and measure the number of steps you take every day. If today you walk 1000 steps a day (that's two bathroom runs and walking to the copier), a 20% increase every month will make a significant difference. Increasing the calories burned will help you keep your resolution. Additionally, if you know that you need visible metrics and positive reinforcement, a pedometer is a great idea.

Next, you might set a goal to reduce your total caloric intake of unhealthy foods by five percent per week. Keep a journal for six months to measure your progress. This allows you to have foods that provide comfort and nourishment with less drastic and self-defeating outcomes. You can find foods that contain fewer trans fats and still satisfy your love of crunchy foods. Measure results that move you toward your destination, those things that, when accomplished, will increase the likelihood of reaching your goal.

You can develop a training schedule that leads to a 5K walk or resolve to complete a year of regular participation on the company-sponsored volleyball team. You are not measuring weight loss, but the behaviors that lead to it. This leads to habits that support a healthier lifestyle and provides positive changes in manageable increments. It also reduces the likelihood that you will cheat or quit.

To ensure success, individual markers are needed. Set, for example, Week 1, Week 3, Week 6, Month 3, and Year 1 goals. Don't stress over the list or decide you don't have time or need to wash your hair, the dog, or the car. Your Month 3 goal could be to complete the Measurement Exercise. Maybe the greatest benefit is the discipline of completing the exercise, thinking about why you selected the milestone, and how you will get there. In six months, you will have reached three or four milestones. Success breeds success. The second round of three, six, and twelve-month milestone settings will be easier. Remember, this is a five-year plan.

MEASURE WHAT MATTERS

"Grit is passion and perseverance for very long-term goals. Grit is having stamina. Grit is sticking with your future, day in, day out, not just for the week, not just for the month, but for years, and working really hard to make that future a reality. Grit is living life like it's a marathon, not a sprint."[67]

To avoid missing the mark on the road to your destination (see *My Cholesterol is 460?*) you will need clear success measurements and deliverables. They tell you how well you are doing and how close you are to achieving your goal. My cholesterol and the gym example illustrate the problem with quantitative measurements. So what should you measure? Determine what you want to change and then measure the *behaviors* that lead to your desired outcome, like an improvement in your overall health. Do not measure what's easy and convenient, such as the number of visits to the gym; measure what's important, such as your resting heart rate and your BMI. (yes you need to look this up if you're not familiar with it).

If your family's intention is to create inheritable wealth through real estate, determine measurements that will help you reach that goal. These measurements should be based on what you know about your family and what you know about you. Metrics can be event based, educational, or experiential.

Should you measure the number of homes with For Sale signs that you and your family visit? This is an easy metric, and isn't your goal to find and purchase a home? No. Your goal is to use real estate to create inheritable wealth. As Stephen Covey said, "If the ladder is not leaning against the right wall, every step we take just gets us to the wrong place faster." That may or may not mean buying a home within driving distance from where you live today. Develop metrics to measure progress toward your real goal, the one you articulated in the beginning.

A better measurement might be to ask your computer-savvy cousin to create a map of housing sales, industry growth, and resale value trends within a two hundred-miles radius. Use the map to create the list of houses you will consider. This metric will take longer to get, but it will give you a better idea of the best places to buy when you are ready. At the same time, you and your spouse can set a goal of increasing your credit scores. This will allow you to take advantage of better real estate deals and competitive interest rates.

Using these metrics, the family can make measurable progress toward the goal of acquiring quality real estate in a way that has long-term sustainability. Everyone can contribute to the goal. The target can be three states that meet the criteria per month, one hundred points added to the credit score, or fifty dollars a year (from your six-year-old) added to the down-payment fund.

It is especially important in the first six months to establish realistic metrics. You're not Superwoman. If you have not exercised since middle-school, don't establish a goal of running three miles a day, four days a week, and completing a half-marathon in five months. It's a setup for failure and frustration for you and everyone who loves you.

Give yourself a due date for each milestone. Put the milestone on your calendar twice: on the date it is due, and fourteen days before it is due. This will serve as a reminder and motivator. Establish an external reward for accomplishing the goals, but remember that the reason for the goal is to satisfy a passion and desire that is greater than the incremental steps.

What gets measured should also be rewarded. Rewards are important markers. They acknowledge effort, discipline, and accomplishments. The measurement system and the rewards must be connected. The reward for achieving an exercise milestone may be a visit to your favorite ice cream shop for a scoop of sorbet or those new running shoes you've coveted.

For the family working on owning a home, you might want to have a "Wishes" jar filled with reasonable individual and family wishes (popcorn night, a pass on doing dishes or laundry, a movie or game rental, or an extra hour of sleep or curfew). When the family achieves its monthly goal, each member can select a reward, or the family can rotate, and each month someone can reach into the jar and take or grant a wish. You'll build commitment and positive family dynamics.

If your goal is to have your artistic talent supply 25% of your income, take 10% of the sale of your first project, even if it's only $1, and buy something that will remind you of your success.

THE "MEASUREMENT" EXERCISE

Set aside time and complete this exercise. Review your goal(s). The important thing is to have metrics that are achievable and will lead you to your destination.

What is it important for me to measure?

Timeframe	Goal(s)	Reward
3 Months		
6 Months		
1 Year		
18 Months		

THE FIFTH KEY

THINGS TO REMEMBER

- Measurements tell us what we value.

- Metrics are an essential element in achieving excellence.

- Practice behaviors that lead you to your desired outcomes.

- Establish realistic metrics.

- Don't measure what is easy; measure what is important.

- What gets measured should also be rewarded.

- Success is tied to well-executed plans with goals and measurements of progress.

CHAPTER 8

THE SIXTH KEY: EVERYBODY'S ALL IN

There are very few goals that do not involve at least a few people. Everyone who is affected has to be infected with the passion to join me, us, and you on the journey.

"The main ingredient of stardom is the rest of the team."[68]

- John Wooden

WIIFM[69] AND WIIFT[70]

"If I can't dance, it's not my revolution."[71]

—Emma Goldman

I believe Ms. Goldman is saying that if there's nothing in it for me, it doesn't matter what's in it for you. When getting others to join you on your journey, remember that most people want to know "What's in it for me?" (WIIFM) You need to share "What's in it for them." (WIIFT) By now, it should be clear that you cannot reach your goal unless you have the help and participation of those around you. Everyone who is affected has to be infected with the passion to join you on the journey.

In the early stages, it is common to hear, "Why are we doing this?" This question tells you that not everyone involved sees a connection between the effort—the daily activities, the programs and processes—and a goal they see as beneficial. The more everyone involved understands the outcomes, the more likely they will embrace them. The more they are involved and clear about what's in it for them, the easier it is to get them to provide support, ideas, guidance, and help. That's why this, the Sixth Key, is so important.

It is likely that your resolution will touch an ever-widening circle of people. The journey will not be limited to you. Everyone involved has to have some "skin in the game,"[72] some investment in the success of the adventure, and some active involvement along the way. A journey that leaves behind or does not tap into those whose lives will be affected is doomed to fail. When people who are impacted by your decisions do not feel included, they are not likely to put much energy into helping you achieve them.

What does this mean to you? If living a healthy lifestyle results in a kitchen counter with fewer candy bars and a refrigerator with more asparagus, everyone is affected. If there is nothing in it for them, no reward that matters, only endless hours of sacrifice, then the plan is destined to fail miserably. You need to articulate the benefit to and for them. This may mean sitting down and including a space in the vegetable drawer for fruit rollups and a place on the counter for Kashi® chips.

If you want to increase the likelihood that your family will encourage your efforts, it is important to include activities that engage everyone. The morning walk can include the dog, which will thrill your son, who usually has this duty. Giving him an additional half hour of sleep may keep him working with you rather than against you.

Because there are only twenty-four hours in the day, you need to find ways to get the stress release you need for your health. If you want your fifteen-year-old daughter to support your goals, you may need to take a yoga class next to her favorite after-school hangout - the mall. People support goals and destinations to which they can relate. If your teenager hates the idea of looking at homes in Iowa, he will resist contributing money to the family's home purchase fund. If your goal of healthy living includes a salad with lots of red, yellow, and green ingredients and your sister dislikes anything that isn't brown or white, she will sabotage your efforts.

"But," you protest, "I'm doing this for them. If I'm healthier, I'll live longer." As true as that is, if others don't see anything in it for them, anything that directly benefits them, you will end up spending more time fixing problems and less time living the life you desire.

As knowledge, understanding, and appreciation for the goal grows, so does the importance of the participation of friends, family members, and colleagues. If your fourteen-year-old says the food choices are "not fair," you need to figure out how to help her join the journey, not wander the wilderness. Maybe she can make the snack choice once a month.

The youngest members of the family can contribute monthly to the family down-payment fund or become "waste watchers." When someone leaves the room, they make sure the lights are turned off and the computers are shut down. For every six lights they turn off, they get a reward that matters to them. It doesn't have to be large or expensive. It has to give them the feeling that they are contributing and that their part in this is valued.

Find ways to incorporate everyone's ideas. Your eleven-year-old may have a recipe that sounds strange, but tastes great and fits into the goal of lower cholesterol and higher fiber. Grandma's fried chicken can be made healthy and tasty.

To bring people on board, make the journey and the destination visible. Talk about it at every opportunity and make it a part of the decision process. Insure that everyone understands the aspirations. The more people who are active witnesses to your goal, the more likely you are to achieve it because visibility is a measure of importance and conviction.

Think of your journey as a train. The perfect train is one that can accommodate the diversity of all riders. It will be filled with cars with seats for those who like to sit, areas to accommodate people in wheelchairs, handles for those who prefer or need to stand, poles for kids who want to spin around, and handrails within reach of the short rider.

The more helpers your train can accommodate, the more likely you will succeed. Everyone needs a space: a seat, a rail, a grip, or a pole. If the goal will affect your family then not only should the journey engage you or you and your partner, it should also have room for children, grandparents, cousins, aunts, and uncles.

The teenager who is learning about housing and real estate patterns brings her enthusiasm to the family discussion. She gathers support from grandparents, neighbors, and friends at school. She convinces her economics teacher to provide information about housing trends. She talks about the family's goals with increasing pride, and that translates into actions that support the goal and fuel her passion for learning.

Want to insure the greatest participation? Make sure:

- Everyone knows where we are headed, why it's important, and what needs to happen next.
- This journey is a part of everyone's walk and talk.
- Everyone is clear about his or her responsibilities to help us achieve success.

Don't stop, however, at those closest to you. The phrase "Everyone Participates" describes a mind-set of inclusion. The number of possible connections is endless. Find ways for as many people as possible to join you on this journey.

THINK OUTSIDE THE FRAME

"The only possible failure would be never managing to find the right role or the right partners to help you realize that strength."[73]

No matter the goal, someone out there can help. Most of us think about help inside our familiar lens; people I know and am related to, neighbors, and close friends. If you expand what's in your view, everyone you meet is a potential resource, client, and/or supporter. Start with your contacts from elementary school. It's possible to find people you knew twenty, thirty, even fifty years ago by visiting online reunion sites. One of my best friends from elementary school is a prominent attorney in my hometown. I found him through a reunion site, and he is now a supporter and resource.

Your high school reunion committee has contact information that may be useful. Your university alumni has groups you can join. The alumni association can also help you find your college roommate, who may unlock countless other resources. Did you join a sorority or fraternity? Even if you have not been an active member, it's not too late. You can connect with the national or local organization. If your resolution is to build wealth through property, you should not overlook this resource. There are at least twenty people in these groups who can and will help you.

What about all those business cards you've collected over the years? A mailing to this group could produce extraordinary results. If you are starting a business and need to barter resources, the business cards that you shoved in the bottom drawer of your desk can be a gold mine.

Want to build a healthy lifestyle? Go to the Health and Fitness Expo or visit several athletic shoe and clothing stores. The woman who looks like you want to look may have great recipes or know of resources that can help you. Don't be afraid to tell her what you need and ask if she knows anyone who can help or if she has any advice. It will flatter her to be seen as a role model and may be just the positive feedback she has been hoping for to keep her focused on *her* journey. She also may have tips for what not to do that can save you hours of frustration. Don't overlook the Internet. Facebook, LinkedIn, Konnects, and millions of other connecting channels are your new your address book.

THE "EVERYBODY'S ALL IN" EXERCISE

Find a quiet place. Answer these two questions. Don't limit yourself to the people who first come to mind. Think about people you've met— friends from school or colleagues from your previous jobs. Ask yourself if the mail carrier, dry cleaner, or dentist might be able to help. The important thing is to identify as many people as possible and figure out how to engage them in the journey.

1) What groups, organizations, associations, clubs, etc. might be a resource?	
Groups	Contacts

2) Who else might be interested in helping me? How can I get them on board?

THE SIXTH KEY

THINGS TO REMEMBER

- Success depends on "all in," making sure everyone who is affected is infected with the passion to join and stay on the journey.

- People support goals and destinations to which they can relate.

- Inclusivity means all voices must be brought into the room.

- Seek help through multiple lenses—friends, relatives, neighbors, and customers, and don't forget the Internet and social networks.

- Everyone involved has to have some "skin in the game."

PART III:

THE LIGHT ON THE PATH

CHAPTER 9

FAITH IN YOURSELF

There comes a day (the earlier the better) when faith is all we have, and that has to be enough.

BELIEVE YOU CAN

"Today be willing to believe that a companion Spirit is leading you every step of the way, and knows the next step."[74]

You've decided to grow and change. You identified your destination in terms that are clear to everyone with "skin in the game," and to a number of bystanders. You have aligned your actions and your words, found individuals and groups to provide guidance and support, and embarked on a journey of continuous learning. You have metrics, timetables, and measurable outcomes to ensure you achieve excellence. All of the tangible pieces of the puzzle are in place: people, goals, activities, and rewards.

Now it is time to make a leap of faith. I love what Patrick Overton, educator, poet, playwright, and speaker says. "When we walk to the edge of all the light we have and take the step into the darkness of the unknown, we must believe that one of two things will happen. There will be something solid for us to stand on or we will be taught to fly."[75]

First, I must tell you that my faith in my ability to fly is still a work in progress. Like many of you, one of the most difficult things is having faith in one's self. Why? Every day you pass signposts that list your failures, disappointments, and all the ways you have let people down. You can recall every failure since first grade or look in the mirror and see the remnants of bad choices. The older you get, the lower everything drops. Your formerly graceful neck is mottled, stretched, and weathered. Your once-quick mind struggles to calculate the 15% tip at the restaurant. You look at your circumstances, review the choices you made as a teenager, remember how you treated people who depended on you, and declare yourself a failure, at worst, and barely capable, at best.

How can you possibly pass down wealth in real estate if, because of your drug addiction, you are now a registered felon? How can you create a healthy lifestyle when cigarettes and sugar are your two best friends? How can you become an artist, singer, or performer when you can't afford to buy toothpaste, let alone paintbrushes or singing lessons?

It is easy to see why you don't have faith in you, your spirit, and your abilities. However, today we're going to take a different path, because it is crucial for you to believe that you can accomplish anything you commit to do, not based on what you have done in the past, but on what you *can* do going forward. As Winnie the Pooh says, "Promise me you'll always remember: You're braver than you believe, and stronger than you seem, and smarter than you think."[76]

This is where you start. The words you speak create the image you see in your mind and the mirror. Stop asking the mirror to point out your flaws. Tell it how fabulous you look for a woman your age that has lived your life. Zig Ziglar said, "You were born to win, but to be a winner, you must plan to win, prepare to win, and expect to win."[77] I say, you were born to be blessed, but to be blessed you must acknowledge your blessings, accept your blessings, and be thankful for your blessings.

Faith in self is the unwavering belief that you are made in the image of the Divinity. It is knowing that you can do things that might have once seemed impossible, because by faith it is possible to do the impossible. Now is the time to build and nourish a deep and intense faith in who you can be.

CONTROL YOUR WORDS

"Words are singularly the most powerful force available to humanity."[78]

Listening to Oprah in conversation with noted self-help author and motivational speaker Dr. Wayne Dreyer, and televangelist and author Joel Osteen, I learned about the meaning behind the words "I am." They discussed how the words you place after "I am" bring whatever follows into your world. "I am happy" brings happiness, while "I am sad" brings sadness into your life. The two words, "I am," have significant biblical meaning.

It is reported in Exodus 3:14[79] that God describes himself as "I am."

Dr. Dreyer says that when we use those words we're addressing God, and in essence asking the Universe to bring into our lives the words that follow. What are you asking God or the Universe to bring into your life? When asked, "How are you?" do you say, "I'm tired." Or "I am fat?" Are you intentionally asking the universe to bring more weariness or fat into your life? Do you really want tired and fat coming to you in abundance? No? Then stop inviting them.

During a recent conversation, a young woman told me she was exercising and eating healthy, yet not losing weight, which was one of her goals. After hearing me talk about the power of I AM, she shared that every morning, she looked in the mirror and said, "I am fat."

I cautioned her that "I am slim" could be accomplished by having an illness or an accident, and that her goal was to be beautiful and healthy, not merely to weigh less. The possibility that she was inviting fat into her life was enough to compel her to change her morning saying to, "I am healthy and beautiful." When people ask me how I am (most know I had cancer), I say with intention, "I am well." I follow that with "I am blessed." If I'm going to call something into my life, I want it to be wellness and blessings.

I witnessed this with my friend Anna. From the first time I met her, it was clear what her dream was. When I talked about women, passion, and courage, she talked about her desire to be an artist. She toured museums in every city she visited and looked at thousands of paintings in books online, at bookstores, and at friends' homes. The day came when, for the first time in her life, she didn't have to struggle to make a living, but even if she didn't have to work to live, she had to paint, sculpt, and create in order to feel alive.

I told her I believed she had to declare her intention if she hoped to move from today's reality to tomorrow's dream. Her divine gift was already growing, and all she needed was the courage to claim it. I shared the principle of I AM and suggested that she begin to say, "I am an artist." We agreed that when anyone asked her what she did, she would say, "I am an artist!" Not "I'd like to be an artist," or "Someday I hope to paint and sculpt," but "I *am* an artist." For my birthday, she sent me a beautiful piece of her art, a 5"x7" portrait of me. The card that accompanied it said, "Thank you! For continuing to inspire women (me). For helping me be who I am—an *Artist*."

Listen to your words and look at your life. If Oprah, Joel, Wayne, and I are wrong, the worst thing that can happen is you will stop saying negative things about yourself. If we are right, this could change your life.

For the next thirty days, before your feet touch the floor, send out some new invitations. Invite some of these blessings into your life.

I am full of health, vitality, and wholeness.

I am prosperous.

I am able and capable.

I am happy and peaceful.

I am a great mother, wife, spouse, or friend.

I am surrounded by God's blessings.

This is the beginning of believing that you are worthy of a joyful life. I intentionally use the word "worthy." To believe you are worth your dream, you'll have to begin to love and honor the person you are right now.

LEARN TO LOVE YOURSELF

"The will of god will not take you where the grace of god will not protect you."[80]

For you to become your best self, you have to love who you are today. For many of you, this is much more difficult than setting a goal, establishing and executing a plan, or acting with courage. You have years of secrets that lead you to believe you are worth so little that you can never have greatness. You are convinced that you will never be blessed because you have committed too many crimes, told too many lies, hurt too many people, and done things that doom you to eternal Hell.

I have done many things I am not proud of. I have stolen, lied, hurt people and animals, disappointed those I love, mistreated people who trusted me, and abused my body and soul. While writing this book, I had to face things that I have hidden for decades. I needed to be reminded that they are my "do," not my "who." They are things I did, but they are not who I am.

I am honest, even though I have stolen.

I am loving, in spite of the times I have been unloving toward others and myself.

I am kind, even in the face of the many times I have been unkind.

I am a good person who has done things I would rather forget.

I am capable of greatness, regardless of my start or position today.

At Prolific Living, I found an interesting and timely podcast titled: *The Daily Interaction: Eleven I AM Phrases to Transform Your Life.*[81] Founder Famoosh Brock gave me permission to share this wonderful list of "I Am" statements. If you get stuck on your thirty days of the "I am" exercise, I hope Ms. Brock's words will provide inspiration.

1. *I am important.* YOU MATTER. Your life, your being here, your contributions—it all matters.

2. *I am happy.* STOP the depressing thoughts. End the endless unhappy cycles. Even if you have issues you are working through, say you are happy and then work through them.

3. *I am grateful.* Be thankful. Don't forget the blessings in your life. This does not mean you won't strive for more. It just means you observe present moment gratitude.

4. *I am capable.* Take a chapter out of Carrie Wilkerson's book on this one and stop saying you can't. How do you know? When was the last time you gave it your all and it failed?

5. *I am strong.* Remind yourself that you are strong. Never say you are weak. Always say and believe "strong." It will start to manifest itself in ways that get you there.

6. *I am full of love and understanding.* Try not to express anger, even in the most difficult situations. It always leads to regret.

7. *I am healthy.* Say it and let it sink in. Then, if you are not exactly there, it helps you strive for it.

8. *I am beautiful.* Or *I am handsome.* Remind yourself and believe it. Beauty is in the eyes of the beholder, and you are that beholder. Believe it.

9. *I am full of energy and vitality.* This is my campaign to ban the words "I am tired." Instead, add words that mean the opposite.

10. *I am hard working.* Believe that you work hard. Lazy has no place in your life or speech.

11. *I am a writer, dancer, speaker, actor, educator, entertainer—whatever you may be!* You must first give yourself permission to be it before others can see you in it.

THE "I AM" EXERCISE

For thirty days, record and read aloud (remember, shame hides in our silence) a positive "I am" statement. You can use the important ones more than once, but not more than three times. When you say the words, mean them, believe in them, and own them. When you hear a negative statement coming out of your mouth, change it! The first few days, it may feel uncomfortable to say "I am powerful" or "I am blessed." By the ninth day, it will feel as natural as blessing your food or greeting a coworker.

Day	I am
1.	
2.	
3.	
4.	
5.	
6.	
7.	
8.	
9.	
10.	
11.	

12.	
13.	
14.	
15.	
16.	
17.	
18.	
19.	
20.	
21.	
22.	
23.	
24.	
25.	
26.	
27.	
28.	
29.	
30.	

FAITH IN YOURSELF

THINGS TO REMEMBER

- The words you speak create the image you see in your mind and in the mirror.

- Believe that you are made in the image of the Divinity.

- Having faith in others is smart; having faith in you is vital.

- The words you place after "I am" bring whatever you say into your life.

- Invite good things into your life.

CHAPTER 10

FAITH IN OTHERS

"I've always thought that people need to feel good about themselves and I see my role as offering support to them, to provide some light along the way."[82]

- Leo Buscaglia

BLANCHE DUBOIS WAS RIGHT

"In everyone's life, at some time, our inner fire goes out. It is then burst into flame by an encounter with another human being. We should all be thankful for those people who rekindle the inner spirit."[83]

In Tennessee Williams's 1947 play, *A Streetcar Named Desire*, Blanche Dubois comes to New Orleans penniless, to stay with her sister and her brother-in-law Stanley. One of her most famous lines is, "I have always depended on the kindness of strangers."[84]

For many of us, depending on the kindness of strangers or having faith in the goodness of others may be more difficult than believing in self or God. Perhaps when you were growing up, the people you looked up to were abusive, dishonest, and awful. More likely, family members were just a disappointment, people who didn't keep their commitments, let you down, and whose actions made you feel unloved and insecure. Every time you think about trusting anyone, you are stopped by painful memories that feel like they happened yesterday. How can you believe in the goodness of strangers when those who were supposed to love you, your family or the people who raised you, treated you so horribly?

To revive your faith in the goodness of others, just look around. There are many examples of the kindness of strangers—the volunteers who suit the women at Dress for Success, the men and women who build homes through Habitat for Humanity, and the thousands who do little things at the mall, in the grocery store, and on the streets of your city.

These fellow citizens confirm my faith in the Divinity, God, and the good in others. Often seemingly insignificant things restore my faith; someone offers to help push the stranded motorist's car out of the road and wait outside for the tow company, or a youngster shares lunch with a child who forgot to bring hers. Here's what I've learned on my journey:

- You can't do it alone. It is not a reflection on your intelligence, perseverance, or commitment. It's just a fact.
- Your network is your safety net. The people to whom you are connected can hold you up when you're struggling to keep your head above water or catch you when you fall.
- Your network increases your net worth. Every friend, acquaintance, and member of your network can help you build, expand, and multiply your net worth. They are invaluable assets. We are all, at one time or another, dependent on the kindness of strangers.

Nothing made this clearer to me than my cancer journey.

THE CANCER JOURNEY

April 11, 2012—I have cancer, and I don't have a job. It would have been easy to stop there. I didn't. I decided to live my cancer as I've always lived my life—out loud and with passion. Two weeks after the diagnosis, I wrote the following letter to my friends and colleagues.

Sent: Saturday, April 28, 2012 1:28:30 PM

I'm finally having to face the fact that I do not control my immediate destiny. I thought I could have the surgery, speak at scheduled events by the end of May, and drive my car home (5,000 miles) beginning June 1.

Yesterday, I met my surgeon. The great news is I like and trust him. He explained that I need surgery as soon as he can arrange for it. I suggested that we wait until after the July Multicultural Conference, but he wasn't feeling it; he actually laughed. I won't be able to do any public speaking for at least three weeks after surgery.

So after four hours of painful tests yesterday (he insisted on knowing exactly where the cancer is and what he should remove—so precise—must be a surgeon's trait), I have finally given up control of my schedule. I'm hoping to have the surgery late next week or early the following week. I will know more on Mon. or Tue.

And for the next week, my email blew up. The messages of love and hope came from close friends and people I'd met only once. Messages like, "You will always be in my thoughts, woman of strength," came from the east and the west. They told me that I was strong at a time when I felt weak and vulnerable.

I knew there was something magical about making my cancer journey public. I was reaching out and connecting from my heart to the hearts of people I'd shared my work with for so long. It wasn't to get sympathy. I didn't feel sorry for myself and didn't want anyone else to, either. I sent my next note on May 18, three weeks after the first meeting with my surgeon.

Sent: Friday, May 18, 2012 1:31:01 PM
Subject: Post surgery

I decided to write this the day before surgery and ask Mendy to send it after I leave the recovery room. I'm hopefully in dreamland, or a drug state that mimics it. :)

I made it through the surgery in my usual fashion—with flare, grace, and my sense of humor intact. All went well, and with the exception of more sutures than I had hoped for, I am on my way back to health and my mission to demonstrate the benefits of living an insanely passionate, courageous, and authentic life filled with laugh-out-loud moments.

In a few days, I'll pick up my Facebook Daily Thanks. Forgive me if I miss days 523 and 524, but I don't know if it's a good idea to post while in a medically approved drug haze. Although I'm not planning to run for political office, I do hope to resume my consulting practice, and what goes on Facebook never stays on Facebook. If you're sitting at home or in your office reading this, everything went as planned. I have blessings and favor, and all the love I've received is the proof.

Thanks for your thoughts, prayers, love, and support. Feel free to share this with others.

Rosalyn

Here's a snapshot of what I received.

"I believe in the power of prayer girlfriend and you have a lot of folks praying for you!!!"

"I am knowing your full recovery and expansion into the next most-fabulous phase of your life."

"I have no doubt that your recovery will be quick, painless, and peaceful."

"I am thinking of you, and your amazing spirit and spunk."

"I know you're going to kick this thing's ass and come back stronger and even more of an inspiration to all of us than you already are. (If that's possible)."

"The BEST is yet to come my friend and we are looking for the message in all of this as we know it will be incredibly Powerful, as God always does."

I felt a tornado of love and support around me. The love, the prayers, and the words of encouragement had a profound affect. For the first time in my adult life, I wanted to spend time with others. I have been very much a loner when not on stage or working. I went to dinner with people if it was part of my work, and if it wasn't, I didn't. The cancer, and more importantly the love, made me rethink that.

Don't get me wrong. I was not happy to have cancer, surgery, a scar, and a shaky future. But cancer put my faith to the test—my faith that God will take care of me, and my faith that I would not merely survive, I would be better, and my faith in my friends, family, and people who loved and supported me. I knew that the "test" was the most important part of my "testimony."

Here was my next note to a growing group of people who cared about me and loved me:

From: Rosalyn O'Neale
Sent: Thursday, May 31, 2012 5:28:31 PM
Subject: Going forward

"I believe that imagination is stronger than knowledge. That myth is more potent than history. That dreams are more powerful than facts. That hope always triumphs over experience. That laughter is the only cure for grief [and illness]. And I believe that love is stronger than death." (Robert Fulghum)

Today my doctors take me through all the test results, and the bottom line is Stage IV medullary thyroid carcinoma.

I realized I had two possible responses. I could go with "STAGE IV—OMG, I'm going to die!" or "I'm okay living with cancer for the rest of my life." As my ninety-one-year-old father says, "You gotta die of something." I am going with the latter. I fly, live in earthquake CA, drive freeways, eat food that has expired, and do all sorts of things that may cause me to come to the end of this session. Cancer has to take a number and get in line.

Next up, medically, I do nothing until Aug. 7, when we see the results of the first set of tests and determine what they can tell us. I have no idea what they will tell me, so I'm not going to work on a plan to deal with the answer. The one thing I am sure of is that I'm not wasting any time or energy planning for the unknown.

Here's what I AM going to do:

1) Heal—My vocal cords are damaged and need time to return to their powerful former selves, and my body has to find its equilibrium again.

2) Enjoy all the gifts—Listen to music, read, drink great champagne and wines, eat truffles, cookies, and candy, take a relaxing spa treatment, drink soothing teas wearing my luxurious Kimpton robe, smell the flowers, light candles for health, and savor the gifts and love they represent.

3) Communicate—Continue my "Thanks on Facebook" (today is Day 534) and maybe start a blog or book based on 500 Days of Thanks.

4) Appreciate—Play with and love Kobe and Noah because every day they make me smile and laugh. Dogs don't worry about "stages." :)

5) Socialize—Have food, drinks, and great times with my friends. So know that any time I'm in your city, I want to have coffee, wine, or Five Guys and share stories.

6) Persevere—Continue to "have the faith that sees the invisible, accepts the incredible, believes the impossible and can conquer anything."

7) Do the work I love—Telling stories and sharing my soul to inspire people to live their passionate lives.

Thank you for your prayers, love, and support on this interesting journey. Feel free to share.

Rosalyn

I received *more* love and prayers. With every note and wish, my faith in my friends and the kindness of strangers grew.

"I just want you to know that I love you and I believe you are bigger than this. I trust that this experience will be a chapter in your book that you will write. Have I told you I love you? I believe you are better than ok! You are perfect!"

"Rosalyn—Just keep believing girl! You are such an inspiration to all of us, and just through your journey, you're giving us all strength!"

"You've already beaten this thing. The Spirits who see all have decided that they are not done with you yet. You've had tough days (that's where we all come in!) but you're strong, authentic, blessed, loved, prayed for, and prayed upon. That will see you through."

The amount of love was my miracle. At this point in the journey, I truly believed that if Stage IV meant the beginning of the end or the end of the beginning, whatever my fate, I would be fine. I did not regret having cancer.

I hear you shouting, "Bullshit! Nobody wants cancer, especially not Stage IV." That's true. I would not have asked for it; still, cancer allowed me to experience the kindness and love of friends, family, and strangers.

I think everything happens when it should—the good stuff and the bad stuff. This was perfectly timed. I had been preaching that you can have either faith or fear, and every day, cancer gave me a chance to choose faith. It brought my words to life and provided the opportunity for love and support to lift me up. For three months I healed, laughed, walked the dogs, prayed, and lived with the knowledge that I would live with cancer forever—and that was okay.

And then came the second miracle!

LOVE CREATES MIRACLES

Next Up:

From: Rosalyn O'Neale

Sent: Tuesday, August 07, 2012 7:47 PM

Subject: Prayer Still Works

My friends,

There's this wonderful song, "Prayer Still Works," by Vanessa Bell Armstrong, and today everything I (and you, and people I've never met) prayed for, came true.

I met with my doctor, and his words were, "Rosalyn, I'm amazed. Your tests results indicate that there is no discernable cancer in your body. I can't tell you how surprised and glad I was when I read the results. I would never have imagined that your results would go from your preop cancer cell levels to "undetectable." If I were to write a book about how I would like everyone's medullary thyroid cancer experience to be—this would be it."

What does this mean? It means that today, it is Rosalyn 1 (Won) and Cancer 0, and I'm going to celebrate the moment with you. I am grateful, thankful, and truly blessed to have my test results, but most of all to have the love, support, and prayers of my friends, colleagues, and family. I think even my dogs were praying. :)

Philip Brooks said, "A prayer in its simplest definition is merely a wish turned Godward." Thank you all for all of the warm and heartfelt "wishes" you sent. This doesn't change anything for me. My plans are to continue to do what I promised earlier:

1. Heal—My voice is stronger every day.

2. Enjoy life—My friends, family, and puppies

3. Communicate—Continue my "Thanks on Facebook."

4. Socialize—Have food, drinks, and great times sharing stories with my friends, beginning this Friday in DC.

5. Persevere—Have faith that these last four months were no accident; they are an important part of my story.

6. Do the work I love—Inspire people to live their passionate lives.

My new business information is in the signature. I'm sure I'll be calling, emailing, and talking with you about what I'm doing and how we can work and play together. Please know that, from the bottom of my heart, I thank you all for your support, your love, and your "wishes."

Until tomorrow,
    Rosalyn

The essence of my cancer journey can be summed up in these two emails I received.

"You are Love and Loved! We are so blessed to have you and now through your story to know that Prayer works. Love heals! Thank you for your Courage, Faith and Strength."

"God clearly wants you to continue to inspire people on this Earth and this part of your story is another part of the amazing and powerful inspiration you give so many people every day."

My cancer gave people a chance to pray for healing and to believe that prayer mattered. And it did! It also gave people I'll never know a chance to feel that God is still in heaven and in charge. Most importantly, it gave me an opportunity to see and be a real, living miracle. It touched me, then you, then them, then all of us. Cancer allowed me to feel love from so many people and allowed me to attract people to love me. Cancer and unemployment affirmed the power of faith in me, faith in others, and most profoundly, faith in God. What did I learn?

Spend time every day healing your heart.

Find something for which to be grateful.

Find someone for whom to pray.

No matter what is going on in your life, you can offer kindness to others. I hope that this book will offer you hope and the opportunity to believe in the power of faith and love.

LIFTED UP, NOT LET DOWN

"How wonderful it is that nobody need wait a single moment before starting to improve the world."[85]

Dear Rosalyn,

What if people have let me down, time after time?

Signed,

Unhappy Susan

Are you like Unhappy Susan? Do you remember every slight? Can you recall each detail of the times people have let you down, but find it hard to remember the times you've been lifted up?

"You don't get it. I've been let down more times than I've been lifted up."

Really? Or does your mind remember the negative more easily than the positive? Neuroscience tells us that our brains are programmed to recall the negative more easily than the positive. However, since it's your brain, it's time to make a space in your head for all the ways the world and others have shown you kindness and love. Here are some examples:

- You're seven, and you forgot your lunch. The teacher, without making you uncomfortable, gives you money so you can buy food.

- You're struggling to get your three-year-old out of the store and into the car. He's having a meltdown, kicking your purse, and preventing you from opening the car door. A teenager gives you a smile and asks if she can help. She takes the keys, opens the car door, and distracts your son so you can slip him into his car seat.

- You're checking into the hotel, and the clerk, without being asked, gives you an upgrade to a bigger room and free Wi-Fi.

- You're shopping at an upscale store for the first time. The sales person lets you have the sale price that won't be available until midnight so you don't have to make an extra trip.

- Your coworker tells the new member of the team that you're the one to go to if they want to see "grace under pressure."

Every time things like this happen, do you add them to the list in the plus column? Or are hurtful things the only memories you keep? We're great at adding up slights and the ways we've been let down and disappointed. Why not begin to catalogue the ways you have been lifted up, made whole, and loved?

I was talking to a close friend, Tina, who teaches in a difficult inner city school. Her students come from homes filled with lack: lack of positive role models, lack of money and food, and most importantly, lack of a future that holds more. She was complaining that her students couldn't and didn't read. At the same time, she decided to start a blog called, "Between the Cracks." The blog talked about how children from these circumstances, who don't learn to read, fall between the cracks of society and seldom reach their potential. I pointed out that she was a kid who could have fallen between the cracks; she came from a home that looked a lot like her students' homes.

"What if," I asked, "God gave you these students on purpose?"

Perhaps, rather than seeing them as an albatross, she could see this as an opportunity to unpack the elements that took her from her circumstances to her PhD. I wanted her remember the good things that happened to her and to share them with her students, to share on her blog how she was pulled from the cracks. To tell her students that they were not burdens, but gifts because they reminded her how God intervened for her good.

Next time you remember a hurt or slight, stop yourself and remember instead something wonderful that happened.

"Nothing good has ever happened to me." Really? What about that job that gave you health insurance just before you daughter got sick? Do you remember the friend who brought you food when you were broke, or the neighbor who used her jumper cables to start your car? The salesperson spent extra time finding the toy your son really wanted for Christmas and gave you his discount so you could afford it. Remember the good times your parents had and not the fights. Recall the fun you had when the city opened the fire hydrants on a hot summer day.

Start to list random acts of kindness: The driver who lets you have the parking space, the receptionist who brought you a glass of water on a hot day. These events build your faith in the innate goodness of people. This faith plays an important part in your journey.

THE "BLANCHE DUBOIS" EXERCISE

Think about Blanche Dubois. "I have always depended on the kindness of strangers." Find a quiet place to reflect. Think of times when others helped you, came to your aid, or provided resources, advice, or love. Start a list and add to it once a week. If you can't think of anything to put down at the end of a week, think harder. Someone let you have something you didn't earn, deserve, or ask for. Someone gave you encouragement or assistance.

For me, this week's Kindness List includes:

- My grandson said, "I love you."
- I received a hotel upgrade to a beautiful room with a view.
- A stranger complimented my hair.

Write it all down and reread it when you need to be lifted up.

My Kindness List

FAITH IN OTHERS

THINGS TO REMEMBER

- Develop your faith in the kindness of strangers.

- Remember the times others have lifted you up.

- Our minds remember the negative more easily than the positive.

- Love, prayers, and words of encouragement can have a profound affect.

- Find something for which to be grateful.

- Start a list of random acts of kindness.

CHAPTER 11

FAITH IN GOD

Faith is the substance of things hoped for, the evidence of things not seen.

– Hebrews 11:1[86]

BELIEVE IN SOMETHING

"Faith is a place of mystery, where we find the courage to believe in what we cannot see and the strength to let go of our fear of uncertainty."[87]

I do not advocate that you share my belief in God. When I wrote *7 Keys 2 Success: Unlocking the Passion for Diversity*, I wanted to put God in the section on Faith. I decided that it was not appropriate to talk about religion in a book written for corporate America. I stand by that decision. This book is different. It is, at its essence, about my relationship with God.

I believe that on a journey to a joyful life, you'll need a power greater than yourself, a power that can do what you cannot. There will come a time when you need to have faith in something: the Universe, a Higher Power, Allah, Buddha, the Divinity—whatever works for you. For me, that power is and has always been called God.

Having faith in God makes my life easier. When my belief in myself starts to wane, or when I feel like others are too busy with their lives, I have Him to talk to and rely on. I would never achieve the joyful life I live without daily, even hourly, help from the Divinity. I ask for big things, like the healing of my grandson Dylan when, at age ten, he contracted meningitis, or a peaceful passing for my mother. I also ask for small things, like great parking spaces. When I've lost my keys, I ask him for them, and they are there. I hear some of you saying, "Come on, Rosalyn; God doesn't care about your keys."

I choose to believe that God cares about the little things and the big ones. It is proof of the greatness of God. I ask God to help people I know and those I don't, and He's always listening. Do I always get my wish? Yes and no. I always get the things that lead me to a blessed life, and I do not get things that are not good for me, or that are not in my best interest. Faith is knowing that at all times, God is listening to me, talking with me, and looking out for me, even in the darkest hours.

BEAUTY FOR ASHES

"Most women 'choose' abortion precisely because they believe they have no other choice."[88]

I was raised in an educated, middle-class, African-American home. On prom night, Ronnie Carpenter, my high school love, and I had sexual intercourse for the first time. About six weeks later, I wasn't feeling well. I thought I had a summer cold. I went to see Dr. Roscoe Bryant, an African-American physician who was also a close family friend. I left his office thinking it was nothing and made the twenty-minute drive home.

As I pulled into the driveway, my mother came out of the house, opened the passenger door, and told me to change places with her. I didn't ask questions. I was raised in the days when a child did not question her mother. As she backed the car onto the street, I asked where we were going. Her reply was short. "We'll talk when we get there." There was an ominous tone in her voice, so I didn't ask any questions.

We pulled into the parking lot of a building I'd never seen. I don't remember where it was; I was concentrating on calming my body, which was trembling in fear. When we got out of the car, she walked ahead, and we entered a dark waiting room. She turned to me and said, "You're pregnant. I'm not going to let you ruin your life. We're going to take care of this."

That's all. Nothing more was said. There was no negotiation, no questions, and no response to be made. It was July 1968. I was eighteen years old, and abortion was illegal.

People do not often talk about having an abortion. Regardless of your position, 1) this is what happens when we're young and impulsive, 2) there are things no one should be subjected to, and 3) it's my life story.

A large Black man, who was not wearing a white coat, came out of a room. He and my mother talked in hushed tones. After a few minutes, he turned to me and said, "Come with me."

I followed him, because there was no voting once my mother made a decision. He had me put on a gown and lie down on the table with my feet in the stirrups. I think it was my first pelvic. What followed was horrifying on so many levels.

He said, "This might hurt a little, but you got yourself into this mess."

Well, that certainly put me in my place.! I was an eighteen year old who couldn't take the pill because the only types available in 1968 made me throw up (which later mimicked morning sickness) and who had the bad luck to get pregnant the first or second time she had intercourse.

He performed a dilation and curettage, also known as a D&C. The cervix is dilated, and the uterine lining is scraped. I didn't have the D&C described on WebMd.[89] I had no "knowing what to expect," no "ease your worries," and no "general or epidural anesthesia." Many years later, I discovered that the "doctor" was a heroin addict, and anesthesia cut into his drug purchasing power.

I do not know how long it took, nor do I have words to describe how much it hurt. I thought I was going to pass out, but unfortunately, I didn't. He packed my uterus, told my mom I'd probably bleed a little, and sent us merrily into the evening. My mother told my father I had cramps and sent me to my room. I don't remember much until two days later.

At about 10 p.m., I started to have severe cramps. I was bleeding heavily. I saw small clots in the toilet when I went to pee. Around 1 a.m., I went to my mother and father's bedroom. I said I was having extremely painful cramps and didn't know what to do. When they turned on the ceiling lights, my gray pallor indicated something more serious. My mother knew what was happening. We got in the car. My father drove and my mother was in the back seat with me. I couldn't sit still; the cramping was excruciating.

When we arrived at the hospital, my mother accompanied me into the ER while my father parked. She told them I was bleeding, and they put me on a gurney and took me into one of the rooms while my father filled out the paperwork.

For four hours, my mother tried to calm me and we waited. The nurse said she couldn't give me anything for pain until the doctor came. I heard my parents ask when they thought the doctor would be there. At one point, my father became enraged.

At about 5 a.m. a doctor arrived. He walked in, dressed in scrubs, a large watch on his wrist and a stethoscope draped around his neck. His brow was furrowed. He examined me then called my mother back into the room and said, "I won't touch her. It's an incomplete abortion." And he walked out. No meds, no recommendations, not a damned thing.

I didn't feel like I had as a close relationship with God. But luckily, He had one with me. His presence came in the form of a wonderful nurse. She bent over my bed, took my hand, and whispered, "It's okay. I've called a doctor who will help you. He's on his way in right now."

Some minutes later, a wonderful doctor came to my rescue. He prescribed a shot to get me out of pain. Then he cleaned up the mess that Dr. Addicted made. Most importantly, when he was finished, he held my hand and told me I would be okay.

Fast-forward three weeks, to the beginning of my freshman year. I am at a school rated in the top five "party schools." I am also painfully sad, ashamed, and unhappy; unfortunately, I didn't know how unhappy I was in any part of my mind where I could have done anything differently.

I smoked cigarettes and pot. I drank cheap pineapple wine that came in a yellow bottle with yellow plastic netting. I had unprotected sex with strangers; some were dates, others just random meetings. I had sex in the snow, beside the railroad tracks, with a guy I only remember as "a very short friend." The sex wasn't good or fun or even interesting, just cold and stupid.

I played cards into the middle of the night, went to sleep at daybreak, got up mid-afternoon, and did it all over again. I was as unhappy as you can imagine and add a bucket more. I went to class only long enough to convince someone to share their notes. I met a man; he was twenty-seven, and to this day, I don't know if he was a student or worked at the school. I knew he was from Chicago, and not much more. Don was not sweet or kind, but he was extremely handsome. He had a brand new car, which he accidentally drove into a frozen lake the night I told him I was pregnant. The two events—telling him I was pregnant and the sinking of the car— were not related to each other, but they were connected to my belief that God would give me whatever I asked for. Minutes before we drove into the frozen lake, I said, "God, I wish I was dead," and God promptly gave me the opportunity. The car sank to the bottom of the lake as I swam to shore and life. I learned God is always listening.

I came home after the December break with a 0.0 GPA. I had five Incompletes. The most incredible thing was that I convinced five professors that I would complete the work and have it to them immediately. We all knew it wasn't true, but I was convincing and convinced.

In September 1969, I gave birth to a beautiful baby girl. The pregnancy gave me a chance to examine my life and allowed me to clean up my act. I gave up most of my vices and began to face the demons that haunted me.

From the beginning of the pregnancy, I knew I would place the child up for adoption. At the time, I didn't know I was adopted, but I was sure of one thing—I would not be a good mother. I believed some family out there could and would take better care of her than I could. God provided me with an incredible social worker who promised to find that family, and she did. I placed her in the care of the State of Kentucky, with a wonderful family, and nineteen years later, we met for the second time.

From the unbelievably awful summer of 1968 to September 12, 1969, the day I gave birth to Katherine Elaine Smith (named after my mother and my best friend), God took the ashes of my life and turned them into beauty. He forgave me and taught me to forgive myself.

If you are carrying the ashes of addiction, prison, crime, poverty, hatred, anger, or abuse, give them to Him and allow Him to turn them into something beautiful. It's not easy, but when I let God be God, it always works out well.

SURPRISED AND AMAZED

"God put us here, on this carnival ride. We close our eyes never knowing where it'll take us next."[90]

I drove along a familiar road on my way home. My sports car carried me past familiar landmarks and businesses. I'd made this trip a hundred times. It's a two-lane road that winds through small New England towns and allows you to avoid the Interstate and traffic.

I rode behind a dump truck. I didn't pay much attention to it. It was old and had obviously traveled these roads before. Fifteen to twenty minutes into the drive, I noticed that the truck's rear gate seemed loose. The potholes in the road caused it to bounce awkwardly. Suddenly, the door swung outward, as if someone had pushed it open, then it dropped to the ground, still tethered to the truck by a chain that was stretched to its limit.

The chain broke, and the large, heavy metal gate bounced once, twice—on the third bounce it shattered my front window. There was glass everywhere. The point of the gate was less than a foot from my face. I pulled off the road and stopped the car. I got out and brushed away the broken glass that was covering the inside of the car and all of its contents, including me.

The driver of the dump truck and several passing motorists rushed to see if I needed help. My overwhelming emotion was surprise. From that day forward, I have been prepared to be surprised. Sometimes the surprise is good, other times not, but I know there are things out there that will astonish me.

On the road to achieving your dreams, prepare to be surprised. It may be at how quickly your business grows, or at the response from a family member. Perhaps it is a contract that you thought you could not win, or a new use for an old idea. A surprise is "a feeling of unexpected amazement or delight."[91] The dump truck gate crashing into my car window did not delight me, but it was unexpected, and it definitely did amaze me. It left me speechless and conscious that things can change in an instant. I am astounded by my successes and my failings, by my great fortune as well as my shortcomings.

On this journey to your joyful life, you may be surprised and amazed by who comes to help or who throws boulders in your way. A friend becomes jealous and says hurtful things about you because she sees greatness in you and your determination. A stranger goes out of her way to introduce you to a room full of potential clients for the same reason.

The flying gate reminds me that at any moment, something unexpected can happen. Do not try to avoid being surprised; you can't. It may not be the flying gate, but I guarantee it will be something as unexpected and amazing.

At least once a week I say to God, "I am amazed." Usually, I am amazed at the awesomeness of God in the little things: I can't find my passport and I know it's in the house, but I've looked everywhere, including all the places it is not nor ever will be. I've looked under the couch cushions, in my closet, in the refrigerator, and under the bed.

As strange as it may sound, in these moments, I'm not stressed, wondering what I'll do if I don't find it, yelling at the dogs, or planning a drive to LA to replace it. I'm not stressed because I'm prepared to be amazed at its reappearance. I remember that He is awesome, and all I need to do is ask for my passport. Within minutes, I find it on top of my desk in plain sight. Was it always there? I don't know, but I do know that He placed it where I could see it, and I'm grateful and amazed.

Do you need someone to help you get your business loan? If you're willing to be amazed, God will place that person in front of you at the grocery store, or their business card will appear at the top of the stack you've been promising to organize. You'll be talking to your neighbor about the best way to keep pests from eating your tomato plants, and he'll introduce you to a friend with a green thumb who also is a retired banker who loves helping new businesses get established.

You must be willing to be amazed. You must be open to serendipity and coincidence; it is a message from the Divinity. You must allow the universe to lead you and direct your steps. And remember that prayer still works.

PRAYER STILL WORKS

"Prayer is taking a chance that above all odds we are loved and cherished."[92]

On Easter Sunday 1999, my father called to tell me that my mother—an incredible, outrageous, and funny matriarch—had suffered a massive cerebral hemorrhage. They'd taken her from Easter Service to the hospital, where she was being rushed into surgery to stop the bleeding. I knew Mom was ready to die, and I knew drilling holes in her skull would mean days of an unbearable headache followed by her inevitable death.

She and my father had been married for fifty-four years. He couldn't just let her go, even though her health had deteriorated and she spent more time in pain than pleasure. She found it difficult to visit friends, have parties and barbecues, fish, shop, or enjoy her great-grandchildren. She was one month shy of eighty-one, and more than ready to leave this life. We'd talked for several years about this time, and her wishes were clear.

She sent me strict instructions. "Do not let them open my chest, head, or any part of my body that would result in severe pain with little likelihood of recovery." She believed I was the only family member strong enough to enforce her will when she couldn't. Problem was, I was in California, and she and all of the voting relatives and friends were in Kentucky.

For the first time in years, I prayed. I did what Joel Osteen says to do when you're afraid, worried, or anxious: "Ask God for a favor." I prayed. I began an intense conversation with God. That day, and every day that followed, I beseeched, petitioned, and pleaded from the depths of my soul for guidance, peace, and a merciful end for Mom.

Somewhere between the first day and the sixteenth, I heard His answers. People often ask if I hear the actual voice of God, and I say, "Yes and no." I didn't hear a voice, but I heard the answers. I don't know how to explain it, but I heard God as clearly as I hear my neighbors— except without sound. God talked to me. He reassured me when I was frightened. He comforted me when I felt the pain of watching my mother's Home Going.

Clementine, who I've known since the first day of high school, says I've always had a connection to God. It didn't feel that way until many years later, but God's always had a relationship with me, even when I wasn't paying attention. With every prayer, my faith grew stronger. It was not simply that my prayers were answered (they were); it was the act of believing in something greater that comforted me.

When she began to weep at the possibility of ending her life in an "old folks' home," I promised her a place in my home, which soothed her, and then I asked God for her peaceful departure from this earth, which soothed me. He answered both prayers. She never went to surgery or any place else. She just sunk deeper into a coma. Sixteen days after she arrived at the hospital, she went Home. The doctors didn't understand how she made it to the hospital alive or what kept her around. I think she was there to reacquaint me with my faith in her, in God, and in myself.

Today, I know that whatever challenges I encounter, I will be fine. I felt this way when I was told I had Stage IV cancer. My faith in others, God, and myself assured me that no matter how it turned out, I would be fine. As my faith grew, so did my gratitude for my blessings. Everyday gratitude is important. It is easy to forget the times I was homeless because today I live in a wonderful home. It is easy to forget that I've been hungry, and it's easy to feel superior to the woman holding the sign, "I'm hungry. Please help me."

Because prayer always works, it's easy to forget that God is the only reason I'm not in prison for driving under the influence as a teenager and an adult. It's easy to forget that on the night I was raped, my throat was not cut. It's easy to forget to be grateful that I was wearing a motorcycle helmet the day the truck hit me. But I'm asking you not to forget. When you're asking God to bring you from your place of pain to a place of blessings and joy, don't forget to say "Thank You."

I am daily and hourly blessed and grateful.

BE THANKFUL DAILY

"'Thank you' is the best prayer that anyone could say. 'Thank you' expresses extreme gratitude, humility, understanding.[93]"

On Thanksgiving Day, 2010, I decided that every day, for one year, I would post on my Facebook page something for which I was thankful. It grew to 800 days and counting, and became a way of life that prepared me for things I could not predict. Why Thanksgiving?

Thanksgiving is one of my favorite holidays. Friends and family fix and eat foods I love: turkey, bowls of cranberry sauce with real cranberries, shaved carrots and pecans or walnuts, and dressing or stuffing (depending on where you grew up) made with lots of sage, thyme, and white pepper—traditional Thanksgiving foods. It's a day of fun, without pressures or expectations.

At many tables across America, it is a Thanksgiving Day tradition to ask each person to share something for which he or she is thankful. In the digital age, I used Facebook as the metaphorical table and posted the following:

Day 1—I am thankful for a God whose love and blessings surround me. Thank You.

From that day forward, I began each entry with the Day and # and ended it with a Thank You (capital "Y"—after all, I'm talking to God with a capital "G"). It may not seem like much, but it forced me to look at my life and my blessings in a new light. Sometimes that was easy; other days, it was a struggle. I included twenty-six of those messages on the following pages. It's a random number, but the posts are deliberately selected.

As you strive to make changes in your life, travel toward a goal of your choosing, and trudge through the inevitable rocky days, be thankful. Find something for which to be grateful. It will make it easier when it's difficult and wonderful when it's easy. If you run out of things, check out twenty-six of my favorites and try to find some inspiration.

26 DAYS OF GRATITUDE

Day 1—I am thankful for God, whose love and blessings surround me. Everything starts with God. I am comforted by my belief that I have a benevolent, forgiving, understanding, and protective Father. My friend Carol would say "Mother," and what I love about God is that He doesn't care. Unlike you and me, He's okay with being called by many names, or coming to people in many forms. He's just light-years better than you and I. Thank You.

Day 62—I was born a "colored" person: that's what's written on my birth certificate. Today, a really good father and husband, a spiritual person, an honorable, intelligent man, and my president, a person of color, stands at the podium, addressing the American people and the world. The distance between "colored" and "person of color" really is a lifetime. Thank You.

Day 65—I'm in Louisville. Sometimes it really is good to be where everybody knows your name, and here that's Rosalyn Kay Smith. Thankful for the original and the new and improved. Thank You.

Day 88—"What you are is God's gift to you; what you make of yourself is your gift to God."[94] Every day, I'm grateful for the chance to be a gift. Thank You.

Day 101—"This is my wish for you: Comfort on difficult days, smiles when sadness intrudes, rainbows to follow the clouds, laughter to kiss your lips, sunsets to warm your heart, hugs when spirits sag, beauty for your eyes to see, friendships to brighten your being, faith so that you can believe, confidence for when you doubt, courage to know yourself, patience to accept the truth, Love to complete your life."[95] (Theodore Roethke) Thank You.

Day 120—Thankful for my dreams: the ones that come with sleep and those that grow and thrive in the daylight. Thank You.

Day 141—I choose to enjoy my life. It is not now or likely will ever be all that I want it to be. But it's pretty damned great! And I think I do You a disservice if I ever forget this. Thank You.

Day 145—God "asked" me to love someone I didn't even like. He told me this was my assignment, no matter how many times, I said, "I can't." He never wavered. I found my way. I really do love "my assignment." It's changed my life. To love someone, to see them as funny and sad, to see the child inside the adult makes me feel good. Thank You.

Day 146—Sometimes I read a post and I am envious of something going on in the writer's life. Then I remember: "Envy is the art of counting the other fellow's blessings instead of your own."[96] And I have so many blessings to count: love, family, friends, work, warmth, and food. Thank You for the reminder.

Day 161—It seems to me that every day I wake up with only two ways to view the day: I can either walk in fear or walk in faith. Fear that I'll lose whatever is important to me, or faith that I will have abundance. I'm choosing faith, and Thank You that so far, so good.

Day 168—"It may be that your whole purpose in life is simply to serve as a warning to others."[97] So here it is: if the pizza's too hot to pick up, it's too hot to put in your mouth. Thankful I can still make myself smile. Thank You.

Day 183—Some days, I have to search for something to write. It seems difficult to identify that for which I'm thankful. Then I realize it because there is so much—not so little. Thank You.

Day 225—To paraphrase Epicurus, don't spoil what you have by focusing on what you don't have. Remember that what you now have was once something for which you hoped and prayed. Thank You for reminding me.

Day 233—I know what I love to do. Seven o'clock Sunday morning, I spoke from my heart to the hearts of 100+ women. What made it so special is I truly love them, and they love me back. It is a blessing I have not earned, and a gift I thank You for.

Day 265—Richard Bach said, "Here is the test to find whether your mission on Earth is finished: if you're alive, it isn't."[98] Thankful I'm not finished yet. Thank You.

Day 277—I'm thankful that every day I get the chance to "do it again" and "get it right." I'm not burdened with yesterday's mistakes or slowed by tomorrow's missteps. Today, I can write magnificent prose on a clean slate. Thank You for the new day.

Day 297—Watching *Man versus Food*, I was reminded: find something you love to do, someone who will pay you to do it, and life is great! Then I remembered. I did, they do, and it most certainly is. Thank You.

Day 318—There is a corner where people's jobs are to hold signs asking for money. Most people don't give anything. They're not sure what the person will buy. I pay them because their job is to help me see my blessings. Thank You.

Day 341—Imagine you are twenty-six, with a ten-year-old daughter. You're best buds. A month later, your child perishes in a house fire three days before Christmas. Today, I helped raise money for Dress for Success so we can continue to help women like this woman rebuild their lives. Don't complain about the noise or the mess or how hard life is; use your blessings and help someone. Thank You for the lesson.

Day 369—The question is "If you had one hour to live, who would you call, and what would you say?" First call, "God, I need more time." The answer, "Rosalyn, I've given you sixty years. Start calling." Thank You for reminding me to stop wasting time wishing things were different.

Day 419—Throughout the day, I've heard one message over and over and again. "Always listen to the voice you hear in your heart. That is the divine message." It's easy to get distracted, to feel like I've lost my way—to forget that I have a divine destiny. Thank You for a day of reminders. You knew that one would not be enough.

Day 453—On those rare days when I am unhappy because I'm not wealthy, not forty (it's amazing how young that seems), not in Long Beach, and not having dinner and drinks with the people I love, I remember the women sleeping on benches at the train station, the families living on the streets, the people whose work is doing the unthinkable, the folks who have no one who cares, and I am ashamed that I can so easily forget my blessings. Thank You for this glorious life.

Day 519—On this Mother's Day, I am blessed to have loved and been loved for forty-nine years by Katherine, my mom, who would have been ninety-four yesterday. I had the good fortune to have two mothers—Lorene, who gave me breath, and Katherine, who gave me life. Thank You for both.

Day 535—Stage IV MTC doesn't frighten me. "I believe that imagination is stronger than knowledge. That myth is more potent than history. That dreams are more powerful than facts. That hope always triumphs over experience. That laughter is the only cure for grief [and illness]. And I believe that love is stronger than death."[99] – Robert Fulghum. I live by faith. Thank You.

Day 678—Most days, I feel like Superwoman—a super human being able to vanquish villains, defeat evildoers, and make the world a safer place for everyone. (Those who know me well are not surprised; it's how I live this life). When they took my blood to perform the test that eighteen months ago told me I had cancer, in the days between "test" and "results," I felt more human than "super." In about two weeks (hopefully sooner), I'll know that it's still Rosalyn "Won," cancer "0." Thank You for the reminder that Superwoman is not Your creation, she's mine (or Marvel Comics). I am Your creation, and for now, human is enough.

Day 713—The question is asked, "If you knew then what you know now, what would you do differently?" My answer is, "Nothing." I would not change one encounter (including the rapist), eliminate any illness—cancer, tonsillitis, or three knee surgeries—all of the ups and downs, highs and lows, pain, sorrows, losses, or joyful moments. All of these bring me here today, and I am thankful for each moment that has brought me to this Rosalyn. Thank You.

THE "FAITH" EXERCISE

For this exercise, it is important to remove all distractions. Answer these three questions. Be as thoughtful and honest as possible.

What would having faith in me look like? What actions demonstrate that I believe in me?

What do I believe about others? What messages do I hear when I think about faith in others? What actions demonstrate that I believe in others? What would I like to change about having faith in others?

What do I think about having faith in a higher power? What messages do I have about faith? What actions demonstrate that I believe in a higher power? What would it mean for me to have faith in a higher power?

FAITH IN GOD

THINGS TO REMEMBER

- There will come a time when you will need to have faith in something.

- God can turn your ashes (difficulties) into something beautiful.

- Be willing to be surprised and amazed.

- Be grateful for your blessings, no matter how small or large.

- Faith is knowing that however things work out, you will be fine.

PART IV:

FINAL THOUGHTS

CHAPTER 12

FROM SEED TO BLOSSOMS

"You are never too old to set another goal or to dream a new dream."[100]

- C. S. Lewis

LET GO OF THE PAST

"Holding on to anger is like grasping a hot coal with the intent of throwing it at someone else; you are the one who gets burned."[101]

At several points along the way, you need to release the past and put it where it belongs—behind you. The only thing you can do is to learn its lessons and let it go. You have no control over it and cannot change it, revise it, or eradicate it. Letting go also means releasing the anger you carry for all the people who have wronged or hurt you. I love Oprah's take on this. She had been angry with someone for months, and one day, she saw that person across the street laughing and having a great time. No pox, no unbearable depression—instead, the person was having a wonderful life. Oprah said she realized that she'd been holding on to anger, and the object of her scorn had gone on with her life.

Releasing the past requires you to make peace with the things that happened to you that you did not deserve—the good and the bad. Is life fair? Sometimes. Sometimes it works in your favor and sometimes not. When it's fair, do you moan and complain? Unlikely. Then why, when it's unfair, do you raise your fists to the heaven and bemoan your fate?

Did the skank in the office get the promotion you coveted? Yes. Did she deserve it more than you? No. Instead of spending your energy being angry, decide that God has a better plan for you around the corner. If you sit on the curb and whine, you'll never receive it. Anger can keep you from moving in the direction of your heart. The time you spend talking about how he did you wrong could be spent preparing for the certification exam that will get closer to the joy you seek.

The energy you spend thinking of ways to exact revenge on the person who cut in line at the store could be dedicated to learning something about human behavior that will benefit you later. While you're calculating the slights you've endured from your neighbors, you could be calculating how to pay your credit cards off and improve your credit rating. Don't spend your precious time and energy worried, fretting, or moaning about the past or being mad at someone who doesn't know you're angry and wouldn't care. You have a lot of work to do on this journey. Make peace with the past. Remember what you have learned, how you've grown, and who you are.

REMEMBER WHO YOU ARE

'My idea of superwoman is someone who scrubs her own floors.'[102]

It's easy to forget who you are, to see yourself in the fun house mirror, and forget it is an illusion. Maybe you want to be like your successful high school rival, or perhaps you think you can do things that no other living person has done and forget that you are human with human frailties and limitations.

You place a big "S" on your workout t-shirt, wrap a towel around your shoulders, and set out to leap tall buildings in a single bound. You want the house on the beach overlooking the ocean. You know your credit is lousy. You know you have no money for a down payment. But that's no problem for Superwoman. You can make the journey from your one-bedroom apartment overlooking a dumpster to the majestic home on the beach in one step. You purchase a listing of government foreclosures from a guy on an infomercial who swears he became a home-owing millionaire in six short months. You buy the list with your one remaining credit card, and when it arrives, it's a cheesy booklet printed on cheap paper. It is filled with information you don't understand, telling you to do things you cannot do, which would not work even if you could.

Maybe in your Superwoman persona, you take on six projects at work with short deadlines (and long odds) the week before your tonsillectomy (substitute any medical condition, significant family event, or family trip).

Your physician (mother-in-law, travel agent) advises you to clear your calendar because you won't be able to talk for three to five days and will need a full week at home to recover. You scoff. They don't know who you are and what you can do. They don't know you're Superwoman.

Now sure, Superwoman, Spiderman, and other fictional characters can make that leap. On the other hand, you and I cannot do the impossible. Don't overestimate your resources, skills, and talents. This mistake costs you time, money, health, and joy.

Perhaps you take on the persona of Superwoman's half-sister, Sharon, the Time Warrior. She can't fly through the air or repel bullets, but she is positive that she can control time. At six in the morning, she is trying to focus on her yoga positions. She's having difficulty because she has work-related meetings and conference calls until 2:45. She also has a meeting across town with her financial advisor from 2:00 until 3:15. Her youngest son has a 3:30 soccer game after school, and she has to pick him up and drop him off. Her daughter has a dental appointment at 3:45, on the other side of town from her accountant.

Sharon is dieting, so she has prepared meals, but they are in the freezer and need to be thawed and cooked. Her daughter wants her to pick up pizza on the way home. Her son wants lasagna from the neighborhood restaurant. She promised to call two clients to discuss her proposals and three parents to talk about the school safety program. She needs to walk the dog, wash her hair, and finish a presentation for tomorrow morning's seven o'clock videoconference.

Twenty-four hours is just not enough to do all the things on her list, so she adds two more hours. She creates Sharon's 26-Hour Day. Sounds silly when you say it aloud, but maybe you've done it. You over inflate time in your mental inner tube, and the result is an explosion that scatters your life everywhere.

Maybe you don't feel like either Superwoman or the Time Warrior but Failing Freda. She looks at what it will take to reach her dreams and sees obstacles looming larger than they really are. "I'll never get a degree. I'm too old, my eyesight is failing, and my memory doesn't work for the small things." The roadblocks seem insurmountable in the face of her frailties. The smallest ruts in the road become the Grand Canyon. Freda's ability to learn, understand, and execute takes a back seat to the size of the task and her fear of failure. Her inner strength is overshadowed by data. She undervalues the power of her will over skill. She's sure she's in this alone. She underestimates the available resources. She forgets that she has friends, colleagues, and associates, who know what she does not know, have strengths that support and negate her weaknesses, and truly want her to succeed.

Remember who you are. You are not Superwoman, Sharon the Time Warrior, or Failing Freda. You are you—human and earth-bound. You are capable, resourceful, smart, and determined, and that is definitely enough.

DEVELOP RIGHT HABITS

"In the European Journal of Social Psychology, *a study showed that it takes approximately sixty-six days to make a habit."*[103]

Along the way, you will need to use *the replacement principle*—replacing a behavior that is at odds with achieving your goal with a behavior that is supportive, wholesome, good, and enjoyable. For example, if you are a compulsive shopper, you know that the slippery path starts with magazines: turning down the pages so you can find it again—a corner here and there. This leads to window-shopping: walking along South Street in Philadelphia, Bond Street in London, or the Mall of America. It builds to the desire to possess that beautiful blouse, those rockin' shoes, or that incredible coat, rather than saving for the home you promised yourself you would buy before your daughter turned sixteen. Building a new habit requires you to first decide to stop the old one immediately.

As soon as you take the magazine out of the mailbox, toss it into the trash. Don't open it. The only place your fingerprints should be is on the outside cover. Put on your current pair of running shoes and take a walk in the park. Read articles in magazines that give you something for your future, not ads that take away your dreams.

The Greek philosopher Aristotle said, "We are what we repeatedly do. Excellence, then, is not an act, but a habit."[104] What do you repeatedly do?

Do you eat healthy or make excuses for the donut? Do you go to the gym, take the dog for a walk, or tell yourself that you will start tomorrow?

It's time for new habits. Replace the donut with an apple and eat it on the way to the gym. Replace the shopping in the mall with a walk around it in the shoes and clothes you already have. No one is looking at you and criticizing your workout clothes, and if they are, you'll be the one laughing all the way to the bank. No one thing we do makes the difference; consistent behaviors will build your confidence and competence.

AVOID THE BACK SPASM

"Your time is limited, so don't waste it living someone else's life. Don't let the noise of others' opinions drown out your own inner voice. And most important, have the courage to follow your heart and intuition."[105]

One reason we try to become someone we are not is we forget the special moments that make us human—the times we are spiritually whole. We are so busy living that we rush through moments that make life worthwhile. We forget that we are physical and spiritual beings.

This is a journey of years, filled with special days and ordinary days. Want to get more out of them? For the next thirty days, take five minutes a day and think about moments in your life when you were fully present. It is important to listen to yourself, to remember what it feels like when you're not focused on *doing*, but on *being*.

Sit quietly and breathe. Listen to the silence, the birds, or the sprinkler in your neighbor's yard. Think about anything or nothing. You're just taking time to unravel the ball of stress that you have become. When you've mastered five minutes, move to thirty minutes a day for thirty days. That leaves you plenty of time to do all the things on your list.

"Whoa! That's extreme! I have children, pets, a spouse, and I am the only person who can take care of everything. I don't *have* thirty minutes."

It's a lot less extreme than a heart attack, divorce, or meltdown. If you don't take care of you, this whole plan falls apart. I hear you protesting. "I'm not a candidate for a heart attack."

Have you forgotten that your stress has been building for years? It started when you were a teenager trying to survive the abuse, find a way to fit in, or impress your family or classmates. In your twenties, it was school, sex, dating, and unmet expectations. Now in your thirties and forties, you're juggling your past and your future with family, friends, work, exercise, and goal setting, and that's just during the summer.

Even if you don't have a heart attack, you're a prime candidate for a back spasm that will reduce you to using a bedpan. You'll be at the mercy of your neighbor, who you know will go through your medicine cabinet because you can't get up to check. Maybe your mom will come by to take care of you, and every time she goes into the bedroom, you're petrified she'll find your stash or that special neck massager. Before you find yourself on the uncomfortable side of the pan-potty, take time to breathe. It takes time to make time. You can't figure out how to create time for the things you enjoy if you don't take time to recharge.

MOVING ROCKS – BUILDING A GARDEN

"When we numb the dark, we numb the light."[106]

This will not be an easy journey. Along the way, there will be setbacks and trials. It is important to face each challenge with courage and faith. I found this out on the road to finishing this book. In the final days, I had difficulty sleeping. I lost interest in the things that gave me joy—going to the gym or walking my puppy Noah. I fought the idea that it was anything other than fatigue. It was the end of what had been a very long year.

I woke every morning with the same ritual. I said thank You for all the ways I was blessed—love, family, friends, pets, financial security, and work that satisfies my soul, but I could not deny that something was off. It was as if I could only be half as happy as usual. I couldn't put my finger on what was bothering me, but I felt like I was just going through the motion. Those who love me would say I had good reason for my dis-ease.

During the last eighteen months of writing this book:

- My job was taken from me. Yes, I wanted to leave the company. Yes, I dreaded going into the office. However, as a person who loves to be in control, I wanted to do it on *my* schedule and in *my* way. It didn't happen when or how I wanted it, and I couldn't do anything about it. I was told that I was no longer needed or wanted. I received a nice going away gift and went quietly, thankfully, and painfully forward.

- I was diagnosed with medullary thyroid cancer and had a surgery that left me with a permanent scar. I was told it was Stage IV, and then told it disappeared. I felt blessed and guilty. Three women I cared about were diagnosed with cancer and they had to survive extremely painful, invasive, and awful treatments. My prognosis was "complete remission." Theirs was not. While finishing this book, my dear friend, Toni Jones, lost her determined battle with cancer.

- My father died. Yes, he was almost ninety-three. Yes, he was ready. He'd lost weight, wasn't eating, and could not play golf or drive, but he was alive, and that meant that every Christmas morning, I could call the house I grew up in and wish him a Merry Christmas. We would joke about his age. He'd say, "I was at the Last Supper," and he would tell me how proud he was of me. Then he'd say, "Well, I'll tell everyone you said hi," which was his way of saying I'm ready to get off the phone. I'd say, "I love you," and he'd say, "I love you, too." I didn't expect this to be in the book.

- My twenty-year marriage to the woman I always believed I would spend the rest of my life with was unraveling. The years of traveling, living in New York and New Jersey, had created a chasm too large to cross.

- I was depressed. I did not invite depression in, but I believe it's important to talk about what is true and not what I want to be true. I had the classic symptoms: loss of joy, appetite, playfulness, and optimism. Joy was replaced by sleep deprivation.

The worst thing was I felt bad about feeling bad. I'd found an incredible group of people for whom to work. I had never been happier with the possibilities work offered. My cancer went into remission, and my father passed quietly away. I knew he was happier and still proud of me. My marriage was deconstructing, rather than disintegrating. We remained loving and kind to each other.

I felt selfish and ungrateful for all that I had. I was angry with myself for feeling anything but happy. My life, by comparison to almost anyone I knew, was wonderful. For a while, I tried to disregard how I felt. Many of you may have tried that strategy. It did not work for me and probably will not work for you, either.

As a part of living a full, passionate, and courageous life, you will have times when your outside and insides aren't speaking the same language. When it's out of sync, the outside looks perfect, but your internal self has jagged edges of sadness. If your outside shows the years and trials, your inside may be calm and peaceful. This won't happen all the time, but when it does, remember that someday soon the inside and outside will be on the same page. In the meantime, get okay with the turmoil and conflict. Denial will not help, so face and acknowledge the truth.

When you find yourself on this road, get help. Find a cleaning person, a therapist, and a friend—two- or four-legged. Acknowledge your fears.

It will take away their power.

- I fear I'm not good enough.

- I fear this idea won't work.
- I fear people will make fun of me.

Acknowledge your gratitude.
- Today, I'm thankful for my home.
- I'm grateful for the sound of my children laughing and playing.
- I'm grateful for the time to paint, write, sing, or plan.
- I'm thankful I can hear the birds singing and feel rain on my face.

To grow the seeds of greatness, you will sometime have to move the boulders, but first you need to acknowledge that they are present and they are heavy. You can't wish them away, but you can slowly and carefully move forward. Remember, "This, too, shall pass." Lastly, continue to grow your blessings.

INCREASE YOUR BLESSINGS

"For today and its blessings, I owe the world an attitude of gratitude."[107]

How do you increase your blessings?

1. Don't sit on your accomplishments, no matter how great they seem in comparison to your friends and family. If you're not moving toward something that moves your soul and makes you smile, shame on you.

2. Be a blessing. Every day, strive to do something for someone else. Be a blessing. Maybe it's as simple as helping someone put their trash in the recycling or carrying their groceries to the car while they struggling with little ones. Be a blessing. Give another woman's daughter help with her homework or self-esteem. Be a blessing. Build someone up. Tell her she looks nice, she's smart, or she's done a great job. Compliment her; it may be what gets her through the day.

3. Keep growing. Dr. Bertice Berry said, "When you walk with purpose you collide with destiny." Read the newspaper. Watch *National Geographic*. Go to the library. Start a journal. Go to Barnes and Noble and read. They don't mind. In fact, they have chairs just for that. Set a one-year goal: decrease your blood pressure, blood sugar, and body fat, or learn a new language. Set a three-year goal: reduce your debt by ten percent, raise your credit score eighty points, save the first year of community college tuition for

your twelve-year-old. Set a five-year goal: build a side business doing what you love, travel to a place you've always wanted to visit, get yourself ready for a "forever" relationship.

4. Be thankful. Thankful requires me to look at what I *do* have and not focus on what I don't have. Be thankful for every trial you have. Millions of folks would trade places in a heartbeat. Be thankful every day for the little things: warmth in winter or the quarter you found in the couch. When you don't feel good, be thankful, because you will feel better soon.

5. Do the last thing God asked you to do. Sometimes I don't want to do what God tells me to do, so I request a new assignment. I say, "God, tell me what you want me to do." The answer almost always is, "Do the last thing I asked you to do, then we'll talk."

The Divinity places seeds of greatness in all of us. The power of passion, courage, and faith is an exploration of how to align your heart and your work with your Divine purpose.

Now it's up to you.

ACKNOWLEDGEMENTS

This book would not have been possible without all the friends, colleagues, and family members who read multiple drafts and provided opinions, feedback, and encouragement. I am eternally grateful to the hundreds of women who shared their lives with me – you were, are and always will be my inspiration.

My life is filled with incredible people who love me and allow me to grow. My father, Charles, taught me that hard work never killed anyone. He also taught me how to make an extraordinary barbecue sauce. Robert showed me the power of unconditional love. Laura for the love and peace I needed to finish this book. Sheila, my best friend for forty years, who can make me laugh at the saddest things and is always there with a pathetic tale of woe to cheer me up. My daughters, Denita Herring and Danielle Barnes, have inspired and amazed me. My grandchildren, David, Dylan, Denisha, and Nate, have pulled me into the future with hopes and dreams of greater times ahead.

I want to thank Jamie Lawson for an unbelievable analysis. Her critique was invaluable. Thanks to everyone who read my drafts and gave me honest and valuable feedback. I am especially grateful to Dr. Clementine Morris, Dr Johnnetta B. Cole and Robby Greg for their encouragement and suggestions and Joi Gordon, CEO, Dress for Success for introducing me to the extraordinary women we serve. You helped me make this so much better, richer, and easier for the reader.

And as I said in the first book, *Unlocking the Passion for Diversity*, I want to thank my mom for teaching me to be irreverent and funny, and I am deeply grateful to God for all the rest.

BIBLIOGRAPHY

Belton, Erline. *A Journey that Matters: Your Personal Lifelong Journey*. Roxbury: Lyceum Group Books, 2008.

Breathnach, Sarah. *Simple Abundance: A Daybook of Comfort and Joy*. New York: Warner Books, 1995.

Brown, Brenè. *The Gifts of Imperfection: Let Go of Who You Think You're Supposed to Be and Embrace Who You Are*. Center City MN: Hazelden, 2010

Buckingham, Marcus, and Donald O. Clifton. *Now, Discover Your Strengths*. New York: Free Press, 2001.

Corcoran, Barbara, and Bruce Littlefield. *If You Don't Have Big Breasts, Put Ribbons on Your Pigtails: And Other Lessons I Learned from My Mom*. New York: Portfolio, 2003

Covey, Stephen R. Th*e 7 Habits of Highly Effective People: Restoring the Character Ethic*. New York: Simon and Schuster, 1989.

Dyer, Wayne W. *Change Your Thoughts, Change Your Life: Living the Wisdom of the Tao*. Carlsbad, Calif.: Hay House, 2007.

Flynn, Jill, and Kathryn Heath. *Break Your Own Rules: How to Change the Patterns of Thinking that Block Women's Paths to Power*. San Francisco, CA: Jossey-Bass, 2011.

Heider, John. *The Tao of Leadership: Lao Tzu's Tao Te Ching Adapted for a New Age*. Atlanta, Ga.: Humanics New Age, 1985.

Hemenway, Robert E. *Zora Neale Hurston: A Literary Biography.* Urbana: University of Illinois Press, 1977.

Hurston, Zora Neale. *Their Eyes Were Watching God: A Novel.* New York: Perennial Library, 1990. Perennial Library, 1990.

Hyun, Jane. *Breaking the Bamboo Ceiling: Career Strategies for Asians: The Essential Guide to Getting In, Moving Up, and Reaching the Top.* New York: HarperBusiness, 2005.

Johansson, Frans. *The Medici Effect: Breakthrough Insights at the Intersection of Ideas, Concepts, and Cultures.* Boston, Mass.: Harvard Business School Press, 2004.

Lewis, Lynette. *Climbing the Ladder in Stilettos: Ten Strategies for Stepping up to Success and Satisfaction at Work.* Nashville, TN: W Pub. Group, 2006.

Pemberton, Steve. *A Chance in the World: An Orphan Boy, a Mysterious Past, and How He Found a Place Called Home.* Nashville, Tenn.: Thomas Nelson, 2012.

Rubin, Gretchen Craft. *The Happiness Project: Or Why I Spent a Year Trying to Sing in the Morning, Clean My Closets, Fight Right, Read Aristotle, and Generally Have More Fun.* New York: HarperCollins, 2009.

Sinek, Simon. *Start with Why: How Great Leaders Inspire Everyone to Take Action.* New York: Portfolio, 2009.

Vanzant, Iyanla. *Peace from Broken Pieces: How to Get through What You're Going Through.* 3rd ed. Carlsbad, Calif.: SmileyBooks, 2011.

Williamson, Marianne. *A Return to Love: Reflections on the Principles of a Course in Miracles.* New York, NY: HarperCollins, 1992.

ENDNOTES

[1] Dress for Success, a global non-profit organization that provides un- and under-employed women with work-appropriate clothing, job interview skills, and career support.

[2] Oprah Gail Winfrey is an American media proprietor, talk show host, actress, producer, and philanthropist.

[3] C. Joy Bell C. (n.d.) "No This Is Not the Beginning." Accessed June 3, 2013. http://www.goodreads.com/quotes/459785-no-this-is-not-the-beginning-of-a-new-chapter.

[4] Anais Nin. (n.d.) "And The Day Came." Accessed December 4, 2006. http://www.brainyquote.com/quotes/quotes/a/anaisnin120256.html.

[5] Graham Dietrich. (n.d.). "Find Your Divine Gift". Accessed Aug. 11, 2014. http://www.findyourdivinegift.com.

[6] Paulo Coelho (Author), Alan R. Clarke (Translator). *The Alchemist - 10th Anniversary Edition.* (New York: HarperCollins, 2009). 23

[7], Brené Brown. *The Gifts of Imperfection: Let Go of Who You Think You're Supposed to Be and Embrace Who You Are.* (Center City, Minn.: Hazelden, 2010). 95

[8] Paulo Coelho. *The Alchemist.* 23

[9] Marcus Buckingham. (n.d.). "Careers Often Go Astray Because People Are Competent At Things They Find Unrewarding."[9] . Retrieved August 13, 2015. http://www.brainyquote.com/quotes/quotes/m/marcusbuck526905.html

[10] Howard Thurmond. (n.d.) "Don't Ask What the World Needs." Accessed March 19, 2010. http://thinkexist.com/quotation/don-t_ask_what_the_world_needs-ask_what_makes_you/346829.html.

[11] Dwana Smallwood. "About the Founder. A Conversation with Oprah Winfrey". Retrieved Jan 5, 2014, from http://dwanasmallwoodpac.org/about-the founder.

[12] Harriet Tubman. (n.d.) "Every Great Dream." Accessed Aug 9, 2012. http://en.thinkexist.com/quotation/every_great_dream_begins_with_a_dreamer-always/346539.html.

[13]Dwana Smallwood. About the Founder

[14] "Shero." Merriam-Webster. Accessed November 8, 2014. http://www.merriam-webster.com/dictionary/shero.

[15] Oprah Winfrey. (n.d.) "Where There Is No Struggle." Accessed April 22, 2011. http://www.brainyquote.com/.../oprahwinfr133739.html.

[16] Alison Rhodes. (5 Nov 2013), [Safety Mom Web Blog]. Accessed Jan 6, 2014. http://safetymom.com/take-two-deep-breaths-laugh-morning.

[17] Maya Angelou. (n.d.) "I Love to See." Accessed May 29, 2009. http://www.brainyquote.com/quotes/quotes/m/mayaangelo578847.html.

[18] Paulo Coelho. *The Alchemist*. 23

[19] Maya Angelou. (n.d.) "Courage Is the Most Important Virtue." Accessed January 11, 2011. http://www.brainyquote.com/quotes/quotes/m/mayaangelo120859.html.

[20] Included with permission from Candi Castleberry Singleton

[21] Lisa Nichols. (n.d.) "You Are the Designer." Accessed January 15, 2014. http://www.goodreads.com/quotes/336022-you-are-the-designer-of-your-destiny-you-are-the.

[22] Arthur Ashe. (n.d.) "Start Where You Are." Accessed April 3, 2010. http://www.brainyquote.com/quotes/topics/topic_motivational.html#zhV7Y38LFgP3 62Fy.99.

[23] Fire Marshall Bill, *In Living Color*. Actor, Jim Carey. Fox Network,1990.

[24] Marianne Williamson. *A Return to Love: Reflections on the Principles of a Course in Miracles*. New York, NY: HarperCollins, 1992.

[25] *How I Met Your Mother* (often abbreviated to HIMYM) is an American sitcom that originally aired on CBS from September 19, 2005, to March 31, 2014 created by Craig Thomas and Carter Bays.

[26] *Basic Instinct* is a 1992 American neo-noir erotic thriller film directed by Paul Verhoeven and written by Joe Eszterhas, starring Michael Douglas and Sharon Stone.

[27] Stephen R. Covey. *The 7 Habits of Highly Effective People: Powerful Lessons in Personal Change*. (New York, Simon & Schuster, 2004) 302

[28] "Courage" (n.d.) In Dictionary.com. Accessed November 22, 2009. http://dictionary.reference.com/browse/courage.

[29] Kenny Rogers (n.d.) "The Gambler." Accessed August 19, 2013. http://www.justsomelyrics.com/1039211/kenny-rogers-know-when-to-hold-them%2C-know-when-to-fold-%27em-lyrics.html.

[30] Bell Hooks. (n.d.) "All about Love." Accessed June 2, 2013. http://www.goodreads.com/work/quotes/270045-all-about-love-new-visions-bell-hooks-love-trilogy.

31 Brown, Brene´. *The Gifts of Imperfection.* 30

32 Brad Meltzer, (n.d.) "The Inner Circle." Accessed November 23, 2014. http://www.goodreads.com/work/quotes/11259924-the-inner-circle.

33 Joyce Meyer is a charismatic Christian author and speaker.

34 Les Brown. (n.d.) "Your Goals Are the Roadmap." Accessed May 24, 2011. http://www.brainyquote.com/quotes/quotes/l/lesbrown385799.html.

35 Michael Egan. *Email Etiquette.* (Cool Publications Ltd. 2004). 32, 57–58.

36 Proverb. "A Stumble May Prevent a Fall" (n.d.) In Thinkexist.com. Accessed June 22, 2012. http://thinkexist.com/quotation/a_stumble_may_prevent_a_fall/149069.html.

37 Gretchen Craft Rubin. *The Happiness Project: Or Why I Spent a Year Trying to Sing in the Morning, Clean My Closets, Fight Right, Read Aristotle, and Generally Have More Fun.* New York: HarperCollins, 2009. 7

38 "Significant" (n.d.) In Dictionary.com. Accessed February 6, 2009. http://dictionary.reference.com/browse/significant.

39 Marcus Buckingham, Assessed April 11, 2016. http://www.azquotes.com/quote-you-will-excel-only-by-maximizing-your-strengths-never-by-fixing-your-weaknesses-marcus-buckingham-79-89-65.

40 Joel Osteen *Become a Better You: 7 Keys to Improving Your Life Every Day.* Philadelphia: Running Press, 2010). 71

41 Greg Anderson (n.d.) "Focus on the Journey." Accessed June 19, 2012. http://www.brainyquote.com/quotes/keywords/focus.html#kIIptalvg8k0cptt.99.

42 A Quote by Lisa Nichols. "You Are the Designer of Your Destiny." Accessed February 20, 2013. http://www.goodreads.com/quotes/336022-you-are-the-designer-of-your-destiny-you-are-the.

43 *The Myth of Sisyphus*, by Albert Camus – A mythical story. Sisyphus is condemned to ceaselessly rolling a rock to the top of a mountain, and it would then roll back down the hill.

44 Bob Moawad. "The Best Day of Your Life." Accessed November 12, 2011. http://thinkexist.com/quotation/the_best_day_of_your_life_is_the_one_on_which_you/8663.html.

45 Stephen Covey. *The 7 Habits of Highly Effective People: Powerful Lessons in Personal Change.* (New York, Free Press, 2003).

46 Joyce Meyer, *Enjoying Everyday Life* Broadcast. Viewed November 17, 2014.

[47] Maya Angelou. (n.d.) "Nothing Will Work." BrainyQuote. Accessed December 28, 2012. http://www.brainyquote.com/quotes/quotes/m/mayaangelo120197.html.

[48] According to Answers.com, this quote is attributed to Eleanor Roosevelt. Accessed June 13, 2013.
http://www.answers.com/Q/Who_Wrote_Yesterday_is_History_Tomorrow_is_a_Mystery_Today_is_a_Gift.

[49] Susan T. Fiske1, Amy J.C. Cuddy and Peter Glick. "Universal Dimensions of Social Cognition: Warmth and Competence." Department of Psychology, Green Hall, Princeton University, Princeton, NJ 08540, USA.

[50] Alfred North Whitehead. (n.d.) "No One Who Achieves Success." Accessed May 5, 2010. http://www.brainyquote.com/quotes/quotes/a/alfrednort119000.html.

[51] Maya Angelou. (n.d.) "When We Give Cheerfully." Accessed September 17, 2014. http://www.goodreads.com/quotes/tag/helping-others.

[52] Diana Nyad. Cuba to Florida Swim, CNN. 8:23 AM EDT, Tue September 3, 2013.

[53] Marcus Buckingham, Donald O. Clifton. *Now, Discover Your Strengths.* 126

[54] Rachael Domenica Scuderi-Ray is an American television personality, businesswoman, celebrity chef, and author. She hosts the syndicated daily talk and lifestyle program *Rachael Ray* and three Food Network series.

[55] Epicurus. (n.d.) In Brainyquote.com. "It Is Not So Much Our Friends Help." Accessed April 11, 2014.
http://www.brainyquote.com/quotes/quotes/e/epicurus161673.html.

[56] Peter Drucker, (n.d.) "Learning Is a Lifelong Process." Accessed November 1, 2012. http://www.albertarose.org/articles/quotes/peter_drucker_quotes2.htm.

[57] Arthur C. Clarke. (n.d.) "Before You Become Too Entranced." Accessed December 12, 2013. http://www.goodreads.com/quotes/110914-before-you-become-too-entranced-with-gorgeous-gadgets-and-mesmerizing.

[58] "Learning Is A Treasure That Will Follow Its Owner Everywhere" .Chinese Proverb . In Quotegarden. Accessed June 17, 2008. http://www.quotegarden.com/learning.html.

[59] "Train" 2004. In Merriam-Webster.com. Accessed May 8, 2004. http://www.merriam-webster.com/dictionary/trainA.

[60] Ibid.

[61] Mahatma Gandhi. (n.d.) "Live as If You Were to Die Tomorrow." Accessed April 28, 2010. http://www.goodreads.com/quotes/2253-live-as-if-you-were-to-die-tomorrow-learn-as.

[62] Tom Peters and Robert H. Waterman. *In Search of Excellence: Lessons from America's Best-run Companies*. Cambridge, Mass. and London: Harper & Row, 1982. 268

[63] Tony Robbins. (n.d.) "Goals Is the First Step." Accessed March 16, 2013. http://morningquotes.net/setting-goals-is-the-first-step-in-turning-the-invisible-into-the-visible/.

[64] Paul Samuelson. (n.d.) "Good Questions Outrank Easy Answers." Accessed June 23, 2014. http://www.brainyquote.com/quotes/authors/p/paul_samuelson.html.

[65] While writing this my father passed away.

[66] *Bridesmaids* Dir. Paul Feig. Perf Kristen Wiig, Terry Crews, Maya Rudolph. Apatow Productions · Relativity Media, May 13, 2011.

[67] "Angela Lee Duckworth on the Key to Success: Grit." Ted Talk, April 2013. http://www.ted.com/talks/angela_lee_duckworth_the_key_to_success_grit.

[68] John Wooden. (n.d.) "The Main Ingredient of Stardom." Accessed July 18, 2012. http://thinkexist.com/quotation/the_main_ingredient_of_stardom_is_the_rest_of_the/342528.html.

[69] Abbreviation for "What's In It for Me?" TheFreeDictionary.com. Copyright 1988-2008 AcronymFinder.com.

[70] Abbreviation for "What's In It for Them?" TheFreeDictionary.com. Copyright 1988-2008 AcronymFinder.com.

[71] Emma Goldman. (n.d.) "If I Can't Dance." Accessed March 11, 2008. http://www.searchquotes.com/quotation/If_I_can't_dance,_it's_not_my_revolution!/222259/.

[72] "Skin In The Game" (n.d.) in Wikipedia.org. Accessed April 3, 2016. https://en.wikipedia.org/wiki/Skin_in_the_game_(phrase).

[73] Marcus Buckingham, Donald O. Clifton. *Now, Discover Your Strengths* 110.

[74] Sarah Ban Breathnach. *Simple Abundance*. (New York: Grand Central Publishing 1995). 30.

75 Patrick Overton. (n.d.) "When We Walk." Accessed June 2, 2011. http://www.elise.com/quotes/patrick_overton_-_when_we_walk_to_the_edge.

[76] *Christopher Robin to Winnie the Pooh*. A. A. Milne. Accessed Feb 2, 2013. http://pooh.wikia.com/wiki/Christopher_Robin.

[77] Zig Ziglar. (n.d.) "You Were Born To Be a Winner" in Brainyquote.com. Accessed November 1, 2011. http://www.brainyquote.com/quotes/quotes/z/zigziglar381983.html.

[78] Yehuda Berg. (n.d.) "Words Are Singularly The Most Powerful Force." Accessed May 7, 2013. http://www.brainyquote.com/quotes/quotes/y/yehudaberg536651.html?src=t_words.

[79] "Bible Gateway Passage: Exodus 3:14" - New International Version. Bible Gateway. Accessed April 29, 2014. https://www.biblegateway.com/passage/?search=Exodus 3:14&version=KJV.

[80] Unknown

[81] With written permission from Farnoosh Brock. Prolific Living, "Episode 54: The Daily Interaction Podcast: Eleven I AM Phrases to Transform Your Life". 2011.

[82] Leo Buscaglia. (n.d.) "I've Always Thought That People Need to Feel Good." Accessed Nov 2, 2012. http://www.brainyquote.com/quotes/quotes/l/leobuscagl120046.html?src=t_support

[83] Albert Schweitzer. (n.d.) "In Everyone's Life, at Some Time, Our Inner Fire Goes Out." Accessed September 19, 2011. http://www.brainyquote.com/quotes/quotes/a/albertschw105225.html?src=t_friendship.

[84] *A Streetcar Named Desire*. The play opened on Broadway on December 3, 1947.

[85] Anne Frank quoted in "How to Make a Difference to the World." Change Your Life, the Change Blog. Accessed April 1, 2014. http://www.thechangeblog.com/how-to-make-a-difference/.

[86] "Bible Gateway Passage: Hebrews 11:1-12" - New International Version. Bible Gateway. Accessed May 14, 2012. https://www.biblegateway.com/passage/?search=Hebrews 11:1-12&version=NIV.

[87] Brené Brown. *The Gifts of Imperfection*. 101

[88] Serrin M. Foster. (n.d.) "Most Women 'Choose' Abortion Precisely Because They Believe They Have No Other Choice." Accessed October 28, 2015. http://www.quotegarden.com/abortion.html.

[89] "Dilation and Curettage". (n.d.) In Webmd.com. Accessed January 24, 2012. http://www.webmd.com/women/guide/d-and-c-dilation-and-curettage.

[90] Carrie Underwood. (n.d.) "God Put Us Here, On This Carnival Ride." Accessed October 17, 2013. http://www.goodreads.com/quotes/tag/surprises.

[91] "Surprise". (n.d.) In Dictionary.com. Accessed March 2, 2011. http://dictionary.reference.com/browse/surprise.

[92] Anne Lamott. (n.d.) "Prayer Is Taking a Chance that Above All Odds, We Are

Loved." Accessed December 1, 2012.
http://www.goodreads.com/author/quotes/7113.Anne_Lamott.

[93] Alice Walker. (n.d.) "'Thank You' Is The Best Prayer that Anyone Could Say." Accessed June 22, 2010.
http://www.brainyquote.com/quotes/quotes/a/alicewalke446395.html?src=t_thankful.

[94] Hans Urs von Balthasar. (n.d.) "What You Are Is God's Gift to You." Accessed May 12, 2012. http://www.goodreads.com/author/show/30796.Hans_Urs_von_Balthasar. 2012.

[95] Theodore Roethke. (n.d.) "This Is My Wish for You." Accessed October 12, 2012. http://www.searchquotes.com/quotation/This_is_my_wish_for_you%3A_Comfort_on_difficult_days,_smiles_when_sadness_intrudes,_rainbows_to_follow/10453.

[96] Harold Coffin. (n.d.) "It May Be that Your Whole Purpose in Life Is Simply to Serve." Accessed September 21, 2013.
http://www.brainyquote.com/quotes/quotes/h/haroldcoff106198.html.

[97] Unknown Author. (n.d.) "It Is Not Our Purpose." Accessed Oct 14, 2013.
http://thinkexist.com/quotation/it_is_not_our_purpose_to_become_each_other-it_is/152509.html.

[98] Richard Bach. (n.d.) "Here Is the Test to Find Whether Your Mission on Earth." Accessed June 1, 2011.
http://www.brainyquote.com/quotes/quotes/r/richardbac101049.html.

[99] Robert Fulghum. (n.d.) "And I Believe that Love Is Stronger than Death." Accessed Oct 21, 2013. http://www.brainyquote.com/quotes/authors/r/robert_fulghum.html.

[100] C. S. Lewis. (n.d.) "You Are Never Too Old to Set Another Goal." Accessed May 14, 2013. http://www.great-quotes.com/quote/196.

[101] Guatama Buddha. (n.d.) "Holding on to Anger." Accessed April 11, 2010. http://www.goodreads.com/quotes/44766-holding-on-to-anger-is-like-grasping-a-hot-coal.

[102] Bette Midler (n.d.) "My Idea of Superwoman Is Someone Who Scrubs Her Own Floors." Accessed August 16, 2014. http://izquotes.com/quote/126773.

103 Phillippa Lally, Cornelia H. M. van Jaarsveld, Henry W. W. Potts, and Jane Wardle, "How Are Habits Formed: Modeling Habit Formation in the Real World." *European Journal of Social Psychology* (2006): doi: 10.1002/ejsp.674.

[104] Will Durant, *The Story of Philosophy: The Lives and Opinions of the World's Greatest Philosophers.* (1926) [Simon & Schuster/Pocket Books, 1991

[105] Steve Jobs. (n.d.) "Your Time Is Limited, So Don't Waste It Living Someone Else's

Life." Accessed August 9 2013.
http://www.brainyquote.com/quotes/quotes/s/stevejobs416854.html.

[106] Brené Brown. *The Gifts of Imperfection.* 81

[107] Unknown. (n.d.) "Today and Its Blessings." Accessed December 1, 2014.
http://thinkexist.com/quotation/for_today_and_its_blessings-i_owe_the_world_an/7511.html.

Made in the USA
Columbia, SC
26 July 2022